Praise

The Unicorn Blueprint" is a game-changer for entrepreneurs aiming to scale their startups into billion-dollar successes. This book doesn't just present theories; it delivers a practical and actionable framework tailored for today's competitive markets. Luis Gonçalves masterfully integrates real-world case studies with cutting-edge methodologies, making complex scaling challenges approachable and achievable. As Saudi Arabia thrives under Vision 2030, the insights from this book are particularly relevant for local entrepreneurs looking to harness the Kingdom's unique ecosystem to build sustainable and impactful businesses. This is more than a book—it's a roadmap for ambitious founders ready to rewrite their success stories.

— **Abdullah Alshamrani**, General Manager of Digital Entrepreneurship Center, Ministry of Communications and Information Technology of Saudi Arabia

The Unicorn Blueprint is an absolute must-read for startup leaders! It offers a practical and comprehensive guide to scaling your business, with a clear framework and real-world examples that make it easy to implement. The Unicorn Blueprint is a game-changer, providing a structured approach to achieving sustainable growth.

— **Basim Almohammadi**, Executve Leader, Raz Group

The Unicorn Blueprint is an excellent new book by Luis Goncales. It is packed with useful knowledge, advice and easy to use and implement templates, all backed by the real-world experience of the author. Every section of description and 'how-to' guides is complemented by case studies of real start-ups and scale-ups which the author has guided and, in the case of both a services business and a product business, built from the ground-up himself.

Reading Luis's book will of course be invaluable for new founders, giving them guidance and a framework for building and measuring every aspect of their new business. Beyond this, the book should be read by all new angel investors, chairmen and early-stage VCs who need a methodology to inspire and support growth and track the progress of their portfolio companies.

— **Rupert Cook**, Chairman, Red Penguin Ventures

If you're serious about growing a business and scaling it to new heights, this book is an invaluable resource. It's not just full of theoretical concepts; it's practical, actionable, and relatable in a way that makes it easy to apply to your own entrepreneurial journey. Each chapter is packed with solid advice, real-world examples, and insights that you can immediately implement to accelerate your growth.

— **Maaly Bukhari**, Founder, Gigsa

What sets this book apart is its holistic view of scaling. Instead of just focusing on growth hacks, it provides a comprehensive framework that addresses everything from talent management to financial sustainability. The real-world examples and practical frameworks make it immediately applicable.

— **Gerard Chiva**, Founder, AKTIA Solutions

The Unicorn Blueprint isn't just another business book - it's a comprehensive guide that fundamentally changed how I approach scaling my company. Every page is packed with practical insights that you can implement immediately. If you're serious about building a world-class company, this is your roadmap!

— **Saeed Alshaikhi**, CoFounder, Tashleeh Pro

Finally, a book that delivers real, actionable frameworks for scaling startups successfully. What impressed me most was how seamlessly Luis weaves together theory and practice, making complex scaling challenges feel manageable and achievable. Required reading for any ambitious founder.

— **Jan-Stanley Brown**, CoFounder, Thakaa Med

Reading this book has been an eye-opening experience for me. As someone immersed in the world of business and entrepreneurship, it provided exactly the kind of inspiration and clarity I needed to think bigger and push further. It's written in a way that feels incredibly relevant to the challenges and opportunities we face as entrepreneurs today. This book is more than a resource it's a spark for anyone with the ambition to build something extraordinary. It left me inspired, motivated, and ready to take my work to the next level!

— **Luke Bodnar**, CoFounder, YamBod Group

Scaling is not just about growth, it's about sustaining the innovation and agility that most companies lose the moment success hits. The Unicorn Blueprint captures this essence perfectly, offering a practical, step-by-step guide for founders and leaders who aspire to build not just bigger companies, but smarter ones. Drawing on real-world experiences and actionable insights, this book transforms complex scaling challenges into manageable opportunities.

— **Abdulmajeed Alaskar**, Founder, MONEYMOON

The Scaleup Methodology is a game-changer for startups. The practical frameworks, especially the seven pillars, offer a clear roadmap that transform abstract startup advice into actionable systems. From sales to product, every chapter builds towards creating an integrated, scalable organization. I love it!

— **Ahmed Al Marjeby**, Co-founder & CEO, Nashid

The Unicorn Blueprint provides what every scaling startup needs - a clear, actionable methodology for sustainable growth. The real-world examples and practical frameworks make it immediately applicable to your business, regardless of industry or stage!

— **Iwo Szapar**, Co-creator of AI-Maturity Index

As the Head of a Family Office representing numerous investors, I have always believed that startups are the lifeblood of innovation. Yet, I also understand the harsh realities of the entrepreneurial ecosystem: 9 out of 10 startups fail. This stark truth challenges us as investors to align our portfolio's growth potential with a framework that effectively mitigates risk. This is why The Unicorn Blueprint by Luis Gonçalves is not just a book to me—it's a strategic advantage.

Luis outlines a transformative methodology, rooted in his extensive practical experience, that addresses the common pitfalls startups face while scaling. For me, this means identifying and investing in companies that are not only innovative but also structurally prepared for sustainable success. This reduces the likelihood of failure and increases the chances of significant returns for our investors.

From my vantage point, The Unicorn Blueprint is more than just a resource for founders—it is a vital playbook for investors. It bridges the gap between entrepreneurial ambition and execution, offering a framework that aligns the goals of entrepreneurs and the expectations of investors.

— **Alla Alenikova**, Head of Family Office

The Unicorn **Blueprint**

Building the DNA of
Billion-Dollar Startups

Luis Gonçalves

SCALEUP METHODOLOGY

First published in Saudi Arabia in 2025

by Scaleup Methodology (https://scaleupmethodology.com/) a brand that belongs to Evolution4all

Contents

Introduction

In the fast-paced world of startups, achieving unicorn status – a billion-dollar valuation – is the ultimate dream. Yet, for every success story that makes headlines, countless promising ventures stumble and fall, their potential unrealized. What separates the unicorns from the rest? Is there a blueprint for building a billion-dollar startup?

These questions have driven my journey for the past two decades, from my early days as a software developer at Nokia to my current role as a global scaleup architect. Through it all, one truth has become abundantly clear: the path to unicorn status isn't paved with luck or chance. It's built on a foundation of methodical, scalable practices that can be learned, implemented, and refined.

But my vision extends far beyond just helping individual startups reach unicorn status. I dream of a world where companies are built to create lasting impact, where success is measured not just in valuations but in value created for society. I believe that if we can successfully spread the systematic approach to scaling that I'll share in this book to startups and accelerator programs globally, we could unlock trillions of dollars in value and, more importantly, accelerate the pace of meaningful innovation and positive change in the world.

Think about what's possible if we could fundamentally transform how companies scale. What if, instead of 9 out of 10 startups failing, we could give them the tools and frameworks to succeed? The impact would ripple far beyond individual companies – it would mean more jobs created, more innovations brought to market, more problems solved at a global scale. This isn't just about building bigger companies; it's about building better ones – companies that can scale sustainably and make a real difference in the world.

A Global Vision for Startup Success

The Scaleup Methodology emerged from a unique confluence of perspectives, drawing insights from both Lisbon's dynamic startup scene and Riyadh's technological transformation. This diverse foundation provided an extraordinary laboratory for developing a truly global approach to scaling startups.

In Lisbon, where centuries of maritime trading heritage meets modern innovation, we witnessed the power of combining historical entrepreneurial spirit with cutting-edge technology. The city's transformation into a vibrant startup hub offered invaluable lessons in evolution and adaptation. Lisbon's ability to attract global talent while maintaining its unique cultural identity demonstrated how local strengths could be leveraged for global impact.

Meanwhile, Riyadh's ambitious vision, with its rapid digital adoption and strong support for entrepreneurship, provided a complementary perspective. The city's emerging ecosystem demonstrated how combining traditional business acumen with cutting-edge technology could accelerate economic transformation.

Working across these diverse environments revealed a powerful truth: while startup ecosystems might differ in their specifics, the fundamental challenges of scaling remain remarkably similar. Whether you're building a company in Lisbon, Riyadh, Singapore, or San Francisco, the core principles of successful scaling transcend geographical and cultural boundaries.

This cross-cultural perspective proved invaluable in developing a methodology that could work anywhere. By observing how different ecosystems approached similar challenges, we identified universal principles that could be adapted to any context. The result is a framework that combines the best practices from multiple startup cultures while remaining flexible enough to work in any environment.

What makes this methodology unique is not where it was developed, but how it synthesizes insights from diverse startup ecosystems into a coherent, practical approach to scaling. It demonstrates that successful scaling isn't about following any one city's playbook – it's about understanding universal principles and adapting them to your specific context.

My Journey: From Nokia's Engineering Trenches to Global Scaleup Architect

My journey in the tech world began two decades ago as a software developer at Nokia in Finland. At that time, Nokia was a global predator, dominating the mobile world. It was during this era that Nokia embarked on its first global agile transformation, providing me with a front-row seat to both best practices on the engineering front and, critically, valuable lessons in what not to do from a business strategy perspective.

This experience at Nokia was just the beginning of a career

that would span multiple industries and roles. Each position I held contributed to shaping my perspective on how successful companies should be organized. However, it also exposed me to a pervasive problem in the corporate world.

Throughout my career in big enterprises, I witnessed firsthand how companies became sluggish and inefficient as they grew, losing the agility and innovation that made them successful in the first place. This paradox of growth became the central challenge of my professional life.

A pivotal moment in my journey came in 2011 when I started my blog. What began as a simple platform to share insights from my varied career quickly transcended geographical boundaries, growing to reach 80,000 monthly readers from across the globe. This success opened doors I hadn't anticipated, demonstrating the borderless nature of digital influence. Despite being based in Germany, my growing audience led to an invitation to write my first book, which in turn catapulted me onto the global stage with speaking engagements at conferences across Asia, Africa, and other continents.

This experience was a powerful lesson in the democratizing force of digital content. I witnessed firsthand how a strong digital content strategy, coupled with an effective digital sales funnel, could not only transform a business but also erase geographical limitations. It became clear that in the digital age, a startup's potential market is global from day one.

A Revolutionary Approach to Methodology Documentation

What you're about to read is not just another business methodology book. In a groundbreaking approach to methodology documentation, this book was co-created through a unique collaboration between myself and Inno Venture AI (https://innoventure.ai/), an advanced artificial intelligence engine for digital product development. This innovative writing process has transformed years of practical experience and deep industry insights into a crystal-clear, highly structured guide that speaks directly to today's startup challenges.

Inno Venture AI (https://innoventure.ai/) represents another ambitious venture we're developing to support startups worldwide in their product development journey. What better way to showcase its capabilities than by using it to help craft this comprehensive guide to the Scaleup Methodology? Through this collaboration, we've not only created a powerful methodology book but also demonstrated the potential of AI in revolutionizing how knowledge and expertise can be transformed into actionable insights.

The Need for a New Approach

The current approach to scaling startups is broken. While accelerators and incubators abound for early-stage startups, there's a critical gap in support for companies at seed and Series A stages – precisely when they're operationally ready to scale. As Chamath Palihapitiya, founder of Social Capital, points out, 40-50% of funding typically goes to marketing – with little to no investment in fundamental business transformation.

This reflects a dangerous misunderstanding of what scaling truly means. Most view scaling as simply pumping money into sales and marketing, but without building robust organizational foundations first, this approach creates devastating bottlenecks. Companies grow their customer base without developing the operational infrastructure to support it, leading to poor customer experience, team burnout, and ultimately, failure.

This broken approach affects everyone in the startup ecosystem:

- Founders waste precious capital on premature growth while neglecting crucial operational foundations
- Investors see diminishing returns as companies hit operational bottlenecks that could have been prevented
- Accelerators continue running outdated programs focused on early-stage growth rather than operational readiness
- Companies face internal collapse as their organizational structure fails to support their growth
- The broader economy misses out on the innovation and job creation that successful startups could provide

In today's startup ecosystem, 9 out of 10 startups fail. This staggering statistic isn't just a number – it represents hundreds of millions of dollars wasted through premature scaling and organizational neglect, along with countless dreams and innovations lost to preventable operational failures.

A Call to Action for the Entire Ecosystem

This book isn't just for founders. It's a wake-up call for investors who should demand more from their portfolio companies and the accelerator programs they work with. The days of accepting mediocre acceleration programs that focus on pitch decks rather than fundamental business transformation must end.

For investors, this methodology offers a framework to evaluate potential investments and guide portfolio companies toward sustainable growth. It provides clear metrics and milestones that indicate whether a startup is building the capabilities needed for long-term success.

For founders, this is about more than just avoiding failure – it's about empowering you to build the company of your dreams, to create something that not only survives but thrives and scales to its full potential.

For accelerators and incubators, it's a challenge to evolve their programs to provide real value in today's competitive landscape.

The Birth of the Scaleup Methodology

Drawing from my diverse experiences across countries, cultures, and organizational functions – including product development, HR, finance, and digital marketing – I set out to create a holistic scaling framework. The culmination of these experiences and insights led to the birth of the Scaleup Methodology in Saudi Arabia's uniquely supportive startup ecosystem.

What sets the Scaleup Methodology apart is its focus on the internal structure, organization, and operations of a scaling company. While many scaling frameworks emphasize external factors like PR, branding, and investor relations, the Scaleup Methodology recognizes that sustainable growth starts from within. It provides a comprehensive approach to building a robust internal foundation that can support rapid external growth.

This unique perspective is rooted in my varied experiences across seven critical pillars of business operations:

1. **SALES:** My journey with digital content strategy demonstrated the power of a well-executed digital sales funnel in erasing geographical limitations and accelerating growth.

2. **CONTINUOUS DELIVERY:** Being part of a startup that lost millions due to an inability to release software made me realize the critical importance of continuous delivery in scaling successfully.

3. **AGILITY:** My 20-year journey with agility, including my role in one of the world's largest and earliest agile transformations at Nokia, has shown me that agility is fundamental for any company starting to scale.

4. **LUCRATIVE:** The financial failures of my own businesses taught me the hard way that mastering the financial aspect is one of the most crucial elements of scaling.

5. **EVOLUTION:** The transformation I led at METRO in 2018, which originally inspired my book "Organizational Mastery," opened my eyes to the importance of a strong governance model for scaling.

6. **UPGRADE:** Helping a company completely revamp its HR department highlighted the critical nature of talent management in scaling.

7. **PRODUCT:** As the engine of every startup, without which the company wouldn't exist, the product pillar ties everything together.

Your Journey Through This Book

The path to building a unicorn is both an art and a science. Each chapter of "The Unicorn Blueprint" unlocks one of the seven critical pillars of scaling success, weaving together theoretical frameworks with battle-tested experiences. This isn't just another business book filled with abstract concepts – it's a practical guide born from real successes and failures in the scaling journey.

As you progress through each pillar, you'll discover:

- Real-world case studies that bring scaling principles to life
- Personal stories from founders who've navigated similar challenges
- Practical exercises that help you apply concepts to your unique situation
- Action-oriented frameworks you can implement immediately
- Strategic insights drawn from successful scale-ups worldwide

Each chapter concludes with a comprehensive Blueprint Summary that transforms insights into action. These summaries serve as your tactical playbook, helping you implement what you've learned in your own organization.

But transformation doesn't happen through reading alone. That's why this book is designed as your entry point into a comprehensive scaling ecosystem. Whether you prefer hands-on learning through our Bootcamp, continuous learning through our podcast, or practical application through our workbook, you'll find the support you need to turn these principles into reality.

The methodology you're about to discover represents not just theory, but proven practices that have helped companies scale successfully across different markets and industries. It's a living framework that continues to evolve with the insights of founders and teams putting it into practice every day.

Let's begin this journey of transformation together, pillar by pillar, as we unlock the secrets of sustainable scaling.

A New Vision for Startup Success

The stakes are high, but so are the potential rewards. By rethinking how we approach scaling from the ground up, we have the opportunity to not just save millions of dollars, but to create value that ripples through entire economies. We have the chance to turn more ideas into world-changing companies, to create more jobs, to drive innovation, and to solve problems at a global scale.

This is the promise of the Scaleup Methodology. It's time to rewrite the rules of startup success, from the inside out. Whether you're a founder with a vision, an investor looking to maximize returns, or a team member in a growing startup, the insights in these pages can help you navigate the treacherous waters of scaling a business.

Welcome to "The Unicorn Blueprint." Let's build something extraordinary together.

Your Journey Continues Online

The concepts in this book are just the beginning of your scaling journey. We've created a comprehensive resource center to support your implementation of the Scaleup Methodology in your startup.

ACCESS YOUR COMPLEMENTARY RESOURCES:

- Practical Worksheets & Templates
- Step-by-Step Implementation Guides.
- Interactive Assessment Tools
- Expert Video Tutorials
- The Unicorn Blueprint Podcast

www.scaleupmethodology.com/resources-from-unicorn-blueprint

Scan the QR code or visit the URL above to access your resources

The Scaleup Scorecard: Your Roadmap to Unicorn

Before we embark on our journey through the Scaleup Methodology, I want to introduce you to a powerful tool that will maximize your learning and growth as you read this book: the Scaleup Scorecard.

Imagine having a comprehensive diagnostic of your startup's scaling readiness at your fingertips - a clear, data-driven picture of where you excel and where you have room for improvement across all seven pillars of the Scaleup Methodology. This is exactly what the Scaleup Scorecard provides.

Available at scaleup-scorecard.com, this assessment is more than just a simple quiz. It's a robust evaluation tool designed to give you actionable insights into your startup's scaling potential. By completing the scorecard, you'll:

1. Gain a detailed understanding of your current scaling readiness

2. Identify your startup's strengths and areas for improvement

3. Establish a baseline to measure your progress as you implement the strategies in this book

4. Receive personalized recommendations tailored to your specific situation

The Scaleup Scorecard is closely aligned with the content of "The Unicorn Blueprint." Each question in the assessment corresponds to key concepts and practices discussed in the following chapters. This alignment means that your scorecard results will serve as a personalized guide, helping you focus on the areas most relevant to your startup's current needs as you read.

I strongly encourage you to take 15-20 minutes to complete the Scaleup Scorecard before diving into the rest of the book. Here's why:

1. **Personalized Learning Experience:** Your scorecard results will help you prioritize which chapters and sections to focus on most intensively.

2. **Clear Goals:** Understanding your starting point allows you to set specific, measurable goals for improvement as you work through each pillar.

3. **Enhanced Self-Awareness:** The process of completing the scorecard will prompt you to reflect deeply on your startup's current practices, priming you for the insights to come.

4. **Maximized ROI:** By identifying your areas of greatest need, you'll be able to extract maximum value from the strategies and tactics presented in the book.

To access the Scaleup Scorecard, simply visit scaleup-scorecard.com and follow the on-screen instructions. The assessment is user-friendly and can be completed in one sitting. Once you've finished, you'll receive an immediate, comprehensive report of your results.

But don't stop there. I recommend retaking the scorecard every 3-6 months as you implement the Scaleup Methodology. This will allow you to track your progress objectively, celebrate your wins, and identify areas that may need additional focus.

Now, you might be wondering: "Is it really worth the time? Do I need to share sensitive information?" Let me assure you: the Scaleup Scorecard is designed to be both time-efficient and respectful of your privacy. The questions are straightforward, and you control what information you share. The insights you'll gain are well worth the small time investment.

Remember, in the fast-paced world of startups, self-awareness and strategic focus can make the difference between stagnation and hypergrowth. The Scaleup Scorecard gives you the visibility you need to make informed decisions about your scaling journey.

So, before you turn the page to Chapter 1, take a moment to visit scaleup-scorecard.com and complete your assessment. Your future unicorn self will thank you.

After all, every great journey begins with knowing where you stand. The Scaleup Scorecard is your first step on the path to building a billion-dollar startup. Are you ready to see where you stand - and more importantly, where you can go?

Take Your First Step Towards Unicorn Status

Start your scaling journey with a comprehensive assessment of your startup. The Scaleup Scorecard will give you a clear picture of where you stand across all seven pillars of the Scaleup Methodology.

WHAT YOU'LL GET:

- Comprehensive Scaling Readiness Report
- Personalized Improvement Recommendations
- Detailed Pillar-by-Pillar Analysis
- Priority Focus Areas Identification
- Action Steps for Each Pillar

Take the assessment now - only 15-20 minutes to complete

www.scaleup-scorecard.com

Scan the QR code or visit the URL above to start your assessment

Chapter No. 1

SALES: Conquer the Digital Frontier

I. The Digital Sales Revolution

It was a sweltering summer day in 2011 when I sat down at my computer, fingers hovering over the keyboard. As a software engineer at heart, I was about to embark on a journey that would transform not just my career, but my entire understanding of how modern businesses grow and thrive. With a deep breath, I published my first blog post.

Little did I know that this simple act would be the first step in a decade-long odyssey, one that would take me from the trenches of software development to the cutting edge of digital marketing and sales. It's a journey that would ultimately lead me to the sun-baked streets of Riyadh, where I now find myself penning this chapter on the revolutionary power of digital sales.

But let's not get ahead of ourselves. To understand the true potential of digital sales for startups, we need to start at the beginning. We need to understand why the traditional sales playbook—cold calls, door-to-door pitches, and glossy brochures—is no longer enough in our interconnected, information-rich world.

In the startup ecosystem, where resources are scarce and competition is fierce, the ability to reach and engage potential customers efficiently is not just an advantage—it's a necessity for survival. This is where digital sales strategies come into play, offering a scalable, data-driven approach to growth that can turn a fledgling startup into a global powerhouse.

Throughout this chapter, we'll explore the key components of an effective digital sales strategy, drawing on my personal experiences and the lessons I've learned—often the hard way—over the years. We'll dive into the power of content marketing, the art of lead nurturing, and the science of conversion optimization

But more than that, I want to instill in you a new mindset—a digital sales mindset. It's an approach that recognizes the power of authenticity, the importance of providing value, and the potential of building relationships at scale through technology. It's a mindset that has taken me from a curious blogger to an international consultant and entrepreneur, and one that I believe holds the key to unlocking exponential growth for your startup.

Now that we understand why traditional sales approaches are no longer sufficient, let's explore the fundamental mindset shift required to succeed in the digital age. This shift isn't just about adopting new tools or technologies - it's about completely reimagining how we think about sales itself.

Let's visualize how digital sales fundamentally differs from traditional approaches:

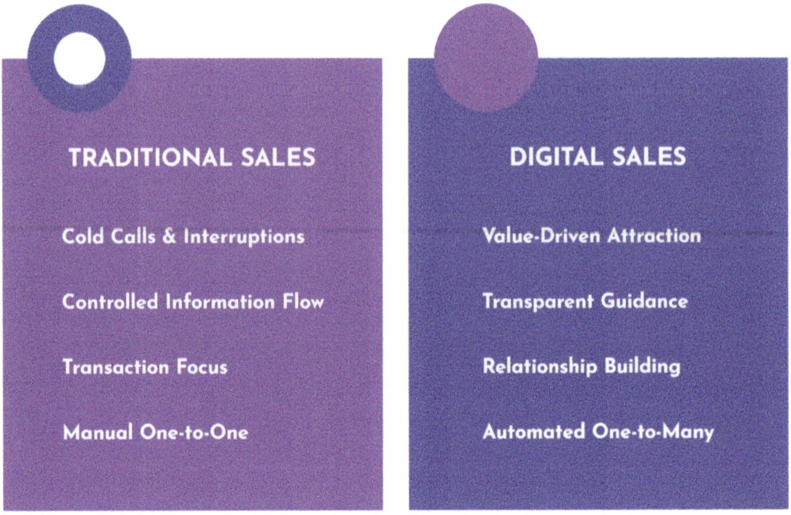

As this comparison shows, each aspect of traditional sales has evolved into a more scalable, value-driven approach. The left side represents the old paradigm of interruption-based selling, while the right side shows how digital sales focuses on attraction and relationship building. This transformation affects everything from initial customer contact to the fundamental nature of customer relationships.

II. The Mindset Shift: From Traditional to Digital Sales

The hardest part of my journey from software engineer to digital sales expert wasn't learning new tools or technologies - it was completely rewiring how I thought about sales itself. Like many technical founders, I initially viewed sales through the traditional lens: cold calls, face-to-face meetings, and persuasive pitches. I couldn't have been more wrong.

Understanding the Fundamental Shift

The traditional sales mindset comes from an era of information scarcity, where salespeople were the gatekeepers of product information. Today's buyers live in a world of information abundance. They don't need someone to tell them about your product - they need help making sense of all the information they already have access to.

This creates several critical shifts in how we must think about sales. First, we've moved from interruption to attraction. Where traditional sales relied on cold calling, unsolicited emails, and advertising interruptions, digital sales focuses on creating valuable content, educational resources, and building communities. The impact is clear: lower acquisition costs, higher quality leads, and better relationships with potential customers.

The second major shift is from control to guidance. Traditional sales processes were rigid, with carefully controlled information flow. In contrast, digital sales embraces a flexible buyer's journey with transparent information sharing. This leads to more trust, faster decisions, and higher close rates. We're no longer gatekeepers of information; we're guides helping customers make informed decisions.

Perhaps the most profound shift is from transactions to relationships. Traditional sales focused heavily on closing the deal - that moment of transaction. Digital sales takes a longer view, focusing on creating long-term value for customers. This approach naturally leads to higher customer lifetime value and more referrals, as satisfied customers become advocates for your product.

Finally, we're seeing a shift from manual to automated processes. Where traditional sales relied on one-to-one interactions, digital sales leverages scalable systems to create one-to-many relationships. This results in better scalability, more consistent customer experiences, and lower costs per acquisition.

The New Sales Equation

In the digital age, the sales equation has fundamentally changed. The old formula of "More Sales = More Salespeople × More Calls" has given way to a new equation: "More Sales = Valuable Content × Efficient Systems × Strategic Automation." This shift has profound implications for how we build and scale our sales operations.

Instead of focusing primarily on hiring and training more salespeople, successful companies now invest heavily in content creation. This means developing educational blog posts, crafting valuable resources, establishing thought leadership, and building vibrant communities. They complement this with robust systems development, including sophisticated lead capture mechanisms, nurturing sequences, conversion optimization tools, and comprehensive analytics tracking.

Strategic automation ties everything together, with smart email marketing systems, advanced lead scoring capabilities, personalized communication flows, and automated follow-up systems. However, it's crucial to understand that automation isn't about removing the human element - it's about enhancing and scaling it.

Practical Implications

This mindset shift affects every aspect of your sales operation. Your investment priorities will change dramatically - you'll likely spend less on traditional sales teams and more on content creation and systems development. Your focus shifts to building scalable infrastructure that can grow with your business.

Your metrics and measurement systems need to evolve as well. Simple sales numbers are no longer enough. You need to track engagement metrics, monitor nurturing effectiveness, and focus on customer lifetime value. These metrics tell a more complete story about the health of your sales operation.

Your team structure will look different too. While you might have fewer traditional salespeople, you'll need more content creators, system builders, and people with strong technical and analytical skills. The emphasis shifts from persuasion skills to the ability to create value and build systems that scale.

Most importantly, your approach to customer relationships fundamentally changes. The goal is to build trust before the first interaction, provide value throughout the customer journey, and focus heavily on education and enablement. Your customers should see you as a trusted advisor, not just a vendor.

Making the Transition

The transition from traditional to digital sales mindset doesn't happen overnight. It starts with education - creating valuable content that helps your prospects understand their problems and potential solutions. This builds trust and positions you as an authority in your field.

Next comes systems building - implementing tools and processes that can scale with your growth. The key is focusing on automation that enhances rather than replaces human interaction. Everything should work together to create a more valuable experience for your customers.

Measurement and optimization become ongoing processes. Use data to understand what's working and what isn't, and continuously refine your approach based on real results. This isn't about perfect execution from day one - it's about constant learning and improvement.

Finally, you need to transform your team. Help your existing team members embrace the new mindset, and hire for different skills than you would in a traditional sales organization. Look for people who understand both the technical and human aspects of digital sales.

With this new mindset as our foundation, we can now turn to the practical task of building your digital sales engine. As my own journey from software engineer to digital sales expert will demonstrate, success comes from systematically applying these principles through a well-structured framework.

III. Building Your Digital Sales Engine

Picture this: It's 2011, and I'm sitting in my apartment in Germany, staring at a blank screen. I've just hit "publish" on my first blog post, and I'm filled with a mixture of excitement and trepidation. At this point, I have zero readers and zero organic traffic. But I have something that, in retrospect, was far more valuable: a genuine desire to share my experiences, both successes and failures, in the world of agile software development.

This was the humble beginning of what would become the engine of my digital sales strategy. At the time, I didn't think of it as a "strategy" at all. I was simply an Agile coach, trying out different techniques in my day job and then writing about what I learned. But this simple act of consistent, authentic sharing would prove to be transformative.

The Four Pillars of Your Digital Sales Engine

Over the years, as my blog grew to 80,000 monthly readers and generated millions in consulting revenue, I identified four critical pillars that form the foundation of a successful digital sales engine.

These four pillars work together to create a comprehensive digital sales system:

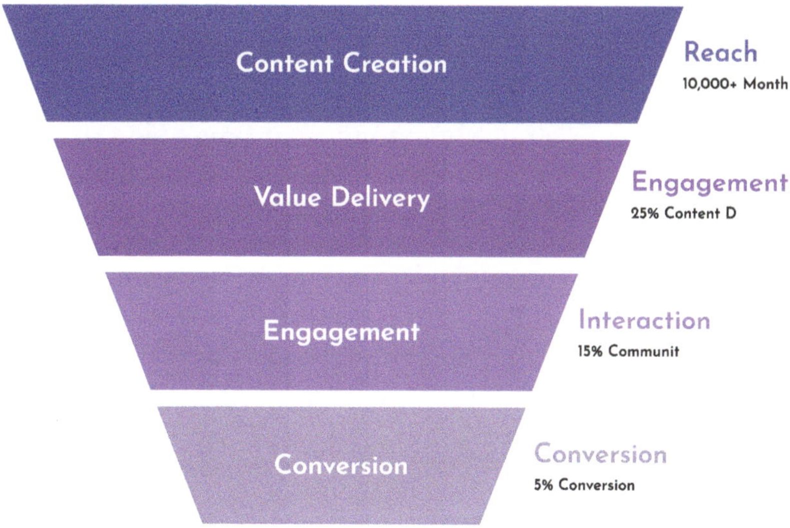

Notice how each level of the funnel builds upon the previous one. Starting with content creation at the top, we progress through value delivery and engagement, ultimately leading to conversion. The metrics on the right show typical progression rates through each stage, highlighting the importance of optimizing each level to improve overall results.

Content Creation and Distribution

Your content is the fuel that powers your entire digital sales engine. But not all content is created equal. The key is creating what I call "compound content" - content that continues to generate value long after it's published. Let me share a concrete example. In 2015, I wrote a detailed blog post about a particularly challenging Agile transformation I had led. The post was honest, detailing both the successes and the setbacks we encountered. It wasn't sugar-coated; it was real. Months later, I received an email from the CTO of a large corporation who had read my post and resonated deeply with the challenges I described. This led to a conversation, which turned into a consulting opportunity worth over €1 million.

What makes content compound over time? First, it must solve real problems your audience faces, not just theoretical challenges. It should demonstrate deep expertise through practical insights while sharing authentic experiences, including failures. Most importantly, it needs to provide actionable takeaways that readers can implement immediately. When content hits all these notes while remaining relevant over time, it becomes a perpetual value-generation machine.

Value Delivery Systems

The second pillar focuses on systematically delivering value to your audience before they become customers. This is where most traditional sales approaches fall short - they try to extract value before delivering it. I learned this lesson the hard way with my first online course. Initially, I tried to sell it primarily through promotional emails and ads. The results were disappointing.

Then I completely changed my approach. Instead of pushing for sales, I created a free email course that delivered genuine value. I developed in-depth guides and templates that people could use immediately. I shared detailed case studies and success stories that demonstrated real results. I offered live webinars packed with actionable content. The result? My next course launch generated €14,000 in a single night - from an email list of just 5,000 subscribers.

Engagement Architectures

The third pillar is about creating systems that foster meaningful engagement with your audience. It's not enough to broadcast content; you need to build relationships at scale. This means developing two-way communication channels where real conversations can happen. It requires building communities where your audience can connect not just with you, but with each other. Every piece of content should invite interaction, and every user journey should feel personalized. Most importantly, you need robust feedback loops that help you understand and respond to your audience's evolving needs.

For example, when I started my "ADAPT Podcast," it wasn't just another content channel. It became a powerful engagement tool that transformed how I connected with my audience. Through deep conversations with industry leaders, I built relationships with potential clients while creating valuable content for my listeners. The podcast generated quality leads while establishing authority in my field, creating a virtuous cycle of engagement and growth.

Conversion Optimization

The final pillar focuses on systematically converting engaged audience members into customers. This isn't about aggressive sales tactics; it's about making it easy for people who already value your content to take the next step. I've found that successful conversion comes from creating clear, value-focused calls to action that feel like natural next steps rather than sales pitches. The path to purchase should be friction-free, supported by authentic social proof and testimonials from satisfied customers. Risk reversal guarantees remove the final barriers to purchase, while strategic pricing tiers ensure everyone can find an entry point that matches their needs and readiness.

Building Your Engine: The Implementation Framework

Now that we've covered the pillars, let's look at how to build your engine systematically across three distinct phases, each building upon the last to create a powerful digital sales machine.

The Foundation Phase spans the first three months, where everything begins with defining your content core - that sweet spot where your expertise intersects with your audience's needs. During this phase, you're not just creating content randomly; you're establishing systematic processes that ensure consistent quality and regular publication. Think of it as building the engine itself before you start the car.

I remember how critical this phase was when building my Agile consulting practice. In those first three months, we focused on setting up the basic infrastructure: implementing analytics to track everything from page views to engagement rates, creating our first lead magnets that would attract our ideal clients, and establishing the email nurture sequences that would build relationships with these early subscribers. Each element was simple but intentional, designed to lay the groundwork for what was to come.

Months four through six mark the Optimization Phase, where data begins driving your decisions. This is when you start seeing patterns in your content performance - which topics resonate most deeply, which formats drive the most engagement, which lead magnets convert best. Based on these insights, you can expand your content types and implement more sophisticated segmentation strategies.

During this phase with my practice, we discovered that detailed case studies about Agile transformations consistently outperformed our more theoretical content. This led us to develop more nuanced nurture paths, customized for different audience segments - one for CTOs, another for Agile coaches, and a third for team leaders. Each path delivered increasingly relevant content based on how subscribers interacted with our previous materials.

The final Scaling Phase, covering months seven through twelve, is where everything comes together and growth accelerates. By this point, you know which content formats work best for your audience, so you can scale them systematically. Your automation becomes more sophisticated, handling everything from lead scoring to personalized content delivery. You're no longer just converting leads; you're optimizing multiple conversion paths for different audience segments.

In my practice, this phase saw us developing parallel conversion tracks - some leads moved naturally from blog posts to webinars to consulting engagements, while others preferred in-depth guides leading to online courses. We built systematic testing processes to continuously refine each path, ensuring we were always improving our conversion rates while maintaining the quality of our relationships.

The beauty of this phased approach is that it prevents overwhelm while ensuring steady progress. Each phase builds naturally on the ones before it, creating a sustainable engine for growth rather than a series of one-off campaigns. Most importantly, it keeps you focused on what matters most at each stage of your journey, preventing the common mistake of trying to do everything at once.

Building for Scale: Systems and Processes

To achieve the kind of exponential growth I experienced with my blog and consulting business, you need robust systems and processes that can scale with your success. Let me share the four crucial systems I've found essential for any digital sales engine.

First is your content creation system. This isn't just about writing blog posts or recording videos - it's about creating a systematic approach to consistently producing high-quality content that resonates with your audience. In my experience, this starts with a well-planned editorial calendar that aligns with your business goals. You need clear templates and processes that ensure quality while maintaining efficiency. For example, when I was building my blog, I created a simple but effective checklist that covered everything from topic selection to final publication and distribution. This system allowed me to maintain quality even as we scaled up our content production.

The second crucial system is your lead generation process. This is where many startups falter - they create great content but have no systematic way of turning readers into leads. Your process needs to encompass everything from creating compelling lead magnets to optimizing your opt-in processes. When I first started, I made the mistake of using generic "subscribe to our newsletter" forms. Once I developed a systematic approach to creating targeted lead magnets and optimizing the entire opt-in experience, our conversion rates tripled.

Third is your nurture framework. This is perhaps the most complex system, as it needs to guide prospects from initial interest to purchase decision through a series of meaningful interactions. I learned the importance of this when I noticed that my most successful course launches weren't to my newest subscribers - they were to people who had been reading my content and receiving my emails for months. Your nurture framework should include carefully crafted email sequences that respond to subscriber behavior and provide increasingly relevant content as people engage more deeply with your brand.

Finally, you need a robust conversion architecture. This is where all your previous efforts either succeed or fail. Your conversion system needs to make it easy for interested prospects to become customers while providing enough information and reassurance to support their decision-making process. When I launched my first course, I made the mistake of focusing too much on the sales page and neglecting the entire conversion journey. Once I developed a comprehensive conversion architecture that included everything from initial interest to post-purchase follow-up, our conversion rates improved dramatically.

Measuring Engine Performance

The true power of a digital sales engine lies in its measurability. Initially, I made the mistake many founders make - tracking everything but understanding nothing. It wasn't until I focused on what I call the "growth metrics hierarchy" that I started seeing real patterns and opportunities for improvement.

Content performance sits at the foundation of this hierarchy. But it's not just about page views and social shares. I remember obsessing over traffic numbers in my early blogging days, celebrating when we hit 10,000 monthly visitors. However, I soon realized that raw traffic numbers meant little if people weren't engaging with the content in meaningful ways. When I started tracking deeper metrics like time on page and, more importantly, content-specific conversions, I discovered that some of our least visited posts were actually driving the most valuable leads.

Let me share a specific example. One of my technical posts about Agile retrospectives only got about 500 views in its first month - a fraction of our usual traffic. However, it had an extraordinary 12% conversion rate for our related lead magnet, ultimately generating more qualified leads than posts with ten times the traffic. This taught me the importance of measuring content performance through the lens of business impact rather than vanity metrics.

Lead generation metrics form the next layer of measurement, but they require nuance to be truly useful. I learned this lesson the hard way when we celebrated hitting 10,000 email subscribers, only to discover that many were unengaged or poorly qualified. Now I focus on metrics that tell the full story: not just how many leads we're generating, but their quality, source, and progression through our nurture sequences. For instance, we found that leads coming from our webinars, while fewer in number, converted at three times the rate of leads from other sources.

Engagement metrics provide the vital signs of your digital sales engine. They tell you whether your nurture sequences are resonating and your content is hitting the mark. But here's a crucial insight I wish I'd understood earlier: engagement patterns matter more than absolute numbers. When we noticed that subscribers who engaged with our case studies within their first week were four times more likely to eventually purchase, we completely redesigned our welcome sequence to prominently feature these materials.

Finally, conversion metrics tie everything together, but they're often misunderstood. Many founders focus solely on conversion rates, but the real story lies in the relationship between metrics. For example, we discovered that while our overall conversion rate was 2%, subscribers who engaged with at least three different types of content (blog posts, webinars, and case studies) converted at closer to 15%. This insight fundamentally changed how we structured our content and nurture sequences.

Learning from Failure: Common Pitfalls and Their Solutions

Through years of building digital sales engines for both my business and clients, I've encountered numerous pitfalls. Let me share the most critical ones and, more importantly, how to overcome them.

The first and most common is what I call "content inconsistency syndrome." I fell into this trap myself early on, publishing frequently when inspiration struck but going silent during busy periods. The problem isn't just about posting frequency - it's about maintaining a consistent voice and value delivery that your audience can rely on. The solution isn't just creating a content calendar; it's building a content system that can operate even when you're busy with other aspects of your business. For instance, I now maintain a three-month content buffer and have clear processes for turning client work and daily experiences into valuable content.

Poor value alignment is another critical pitfall, and it's particularly dangerous because it often goes unnoticed until it's caused significant damage. I worked with a startup that was producing beautiful content and getting decent traffic, but their conversion rates were abysmal. When we dug deeper, we discovered they were attracting the wrong audience because their content wasn't aligned with their actual value proposition. The solution was to develop a clear value alignment framework that ensured every piece of content directly connected to their core offering and target customer needs.

Weak nurture sequences are perhaps the most expensive pitfall in terms of lost opportunity. Many startups either overwhelm new subscribers with aggressive sales messages or neglect them with infrequent, generic communications. The key is building what I call "value-first nurture paths" - sequences that focus on delivering increasing value while naturally leading to your offerings. When we implemented this approach for one client, their sales cycle shortened by 40% because prospects were better educated and more qualified by the time they spoke with sales.

Finally, ineffective conversion paths can undermine even the best content and nurture efforts. I see many startups focus on optimizing individual elements like call-to-action buttons or headlines while ignoring the overall conversion journey. The solution is to map and optimize the entire path from first touch to purchase, ensuring each step builds naturally on the previous one. For example, we found that adding social proof elements throughout the journey, not just on sales pages, increased overall conversion rates by 25%.

While the engine provides the structure, the fuel that powers it is value delivery. Let me share how I learned this lesson the hard way, and how it transformed my approach to digital sales.

IV. The Value Delivery System

Let me share a pivotal moment in my journey that transformed how I think about value delivery in the digital age. In 2014, I was preparing to launch my first major online course about Agile methodologies. My initial plan was typical: create the course, set up a sales page, and start promoting it. But a conversation with a potential customer changed everything.

"Why should I trust your course?" she asked. "There are dozens of Agile courses out there. What makes yours different?"

That question led me to completely reimagine my approach to value delivery. I realized that in the digital age, the sale isn't the beginning of value delivery - it's a natural outcome of value already delivered.

The Value-First Approach

Over the next six months, instead of focusing on selling my course, I focused on delivering value first. I created detailed blog posts about Agile implementation challenges. I shared real case studies from my consulting work. I offered free templates and tools that teams could use immediately. I hosted weekly Q&A sessions where I answered specific questions from my audience.

The results were transformative. When I finally launched the course, it generated €14,000 in sales on the first day. But more importantly, the students were better prepared to succeed because they had already implemented some of my methods through the free content. They weren't buying an unknown promise - they were investing in proven value.

This experience taught me a fundamental truth about digital value delivery: it's not about creating a single valuable product or service - it's about building a systematic approach to delivering value at every stage of the customer journey.

The Four Layers of Digital Value

Through years of refining this approach, I've identified four distinct layers of value delivery that work together to create a compelling digital presence.

Let's examine how these layers build upon each other to create escalating value:

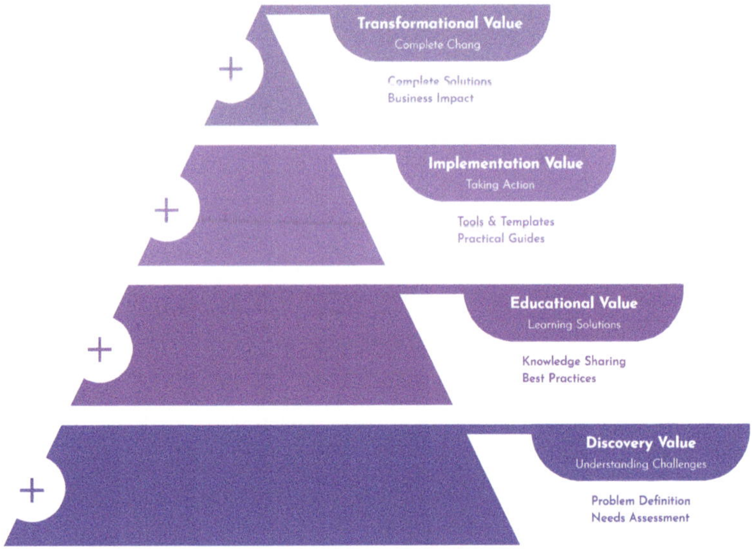

This pyramid structure illustrates the progressive nature of value delivery. Notice how each layer builds upon the previous one, creating an increasingly valuable relationship with your audience. The percentages shown indicate typical engagement rates at each level, demonstrating how value delivery naturally qualifies and segments your audience.

1. Discovery Value The first layer focuses on helping your audience understand and define their challenges. This isn't about promoting your solution - it's about bringing clarity to their situation. For example, I created a free Agile Assessment Tool that helped teams identify their specific challenges before they even considered hiring me or buying my courses. This tool alone generated over 5,000 qualified leads because it delivered immediate value while naturally leading to my more comprehensive solutions.

2. Educational Value The second layer involves helping your audience understand potential solutions to their challenges. In my case, this meant creating detailed guides about different Agile practices, comparative

analyses of various methodologies, and case studies showing real-world implementations. The key is to be genuinely helpful without holding back valuable insights for paying customers.

3. Implementation Value The third layer provides practical tools and resources that help your audience take action. These aren't stripped-down versions of your paid offerings - they're complete solutions for specific problems. My most successful lead magnet was a comprehensive template for running Agile retrospectives. It was so valuable that teams could use it immediately, yet it naturally led them to want more advanced guidance through my paid offerings.
4. Transformational Value The final layer is where your paid products and services create fundamental transformations for your customers. The key is that by the time someone reaches this layer, they've already received so much value from your free content that purchasing feels like a natural next step rather than a risky decision.

Building Your Value Delivery System

Let me walk you through how to build a systematic approach to value delivery, using lessons from my own journey and those of companies I've advised.

First, you need to map your value ecosystem. This isn't just about listing your products and services - it's about understanding the entire journey your customers take. For instance, when I mapped my ecosystem, I realized that teams typically went through four stages in their Agile journey:

- Recognizing the need for change

- Understanding Agile principles
- Implementing basic practices
- Scaling and optimizing their approach

I then created specific value offerings for each stage:

- Assessment tools for the recognition stage
- Educational content for the understanding stage
- Templates and guides for the implementation stage
- Consulting and courses for the scaling stage

Next, you need to create value bridges - content and tools that naturally lead from one stage to the next. These aren't aggressive sales tactics; they're logical next steps that help people progress in their journey. When someone downloads my retrospective template, they automatically receive a sequence of emails showing advanced techniques they can use with the template. These emails don't push my course; they provide additional value while naturally demonstrating the benefits of more comprehensive training.

The key to effective value delivery is what I call the "value compounding effect." Each piece of content or tool you create should build upon previous value and set the stage for future value. For example, my blog posts often reference free tools, which then connect to case studies, which naturally lead to webinars, which ultimately demonstrate the need for comprehensive training or consulting.

Measuring Value Delivery

One crucial lesson I've learned is the importance of measuring not just traditional metrics like page views or downloads, but actual value delivery. Here's how I approach this:

Immediate Value Metrics:

- Implementation rates of free tools
- Completion rates of guides and tutorials
- Active participation in community discussions
- Direct feedback and testimonials

Long-term Value Metrics:

- Return visits to content
- Progression through value stages
- Referral rates from existing audience
- Community growth and engagement

The most important metric, however, is what I call the "value velocity" - how quickly and effectively people can implement what you're teaching or providing. When we focused on improving this metric, everything else improved: engagement rates, conversion rates, and most importantly, customer success rates.

A robust value delivery system is only effective when it's precisely targeted at the right audience. This brings us to perhaps the most crucial element of digital sales success: truly understanding and nurturing your audience.

V. Understanding and Nurturing Your Audience

As my blog's readership grew to 80,000 monthly visitors, I made a crucial discovery that would fundamentally change my approach to digital sales. While having a large audience was gratifying, I realized I was missing something critical: I had readers, but I didn't truly understand them. More importantly, I had no systematic way to turn that understanding into meaningful relationships.

Let me share a story that illustrates this point perfectly. In 2014, I was regularly publishing detailed technical posts about Agile methodologies. The traffic was good, engagement was high, but something wasn't clicking. Then I received an email from a CTO that changed everything. He wrote, "Your posts are technically excellent, but what I really need is help convincing my board that Agile is worth the investment."

This single email revealed a blind spot in my understanding. I had been writing for practitioners when many of my most valuable readers were actually decision-makers facing completely different challenges. This realization led me to develop what I now call the "Understand and Nurture" framework.

The Audience Understanding Matrix

The first step in this framework is moving beyond basic demographics to understand your audience at three crucial levels:

1. **Surface Level:** Who They Are Initially, I thought I was writing for developers and Scrum Masters. But when I dug deeper into my audience data, I discovered three distinct groups:

    - Practitioners seeking tactical guidance
    - Middle managers looking for implementation strategies
    - Executives needing business cases and ROI data

Each group was reading the same content but looking for different insights. Understanding this changed everything about how I created and structured my content.

2. **Middle Level:** What They Need The next level involves understanding the specific challenges and aspirations of each group. Through surveys, interviews, and analyzing thousands of comments and emails, I discovered that:

    - Practitioners needed practical tools and templates
    - Managers needed change management strategies
    - Executives needed risk mitigation frameworks and ROI models

This understanding allowed me to create targeted content that resonated deeply with each group.

3. **Deep Level:** Why They Need It The deepest level of understanding involves the underlying motivations and fears driving your audience. For example, I discovered that while executives asked about ROI, their real concern was often about maintaining control during an Agile transformation. This insight led me to create content addressing the balance between autonomy and oversight in Agile organizations.

From Understanding to Nurturing

Understanding your audience is only the first step. The real magic happens when you turn that understanding into systematic nurturing. Here's how I transformed my approach:

1. The Welcome Journey I completely redesigned my welcome sequence based on audience understanding.

Instead of a generic series of emails, new subscribers now receive a question asking about their primary role. Their response triggers a tailored welcome sequence that addresses their specific needs and challenges.

For example, when a senior leader signs up, they receive a sequence focused on strategic implementation and change management. A practitioner receives more tactical content focused on daily Agile practices. This personalization increased our email engagement rates by over 150%.

2. The Value Ladder Next, I created what I call a "value ladder" - a systematic way of delivering increasingly valuable content aligned with each audience segment's journey. This isn't about immediately pushing products; it's about gradually demonstrating deeper value.

Here's how it worked for one executive subscriber:

- **Week 1:** Received an Agile Readiness Assessment tool
- **Week 2:** Got access to a case study about successful enterprise Agile transformation
- **Week 3:** Invited to a webinar on managing Agile transformations
- **Week 4:** Offered a consultation to discuss their specific challenges

The key is that each step provided standalone value while naturally leading to the next level of engagement.

3. The Engagement Spiral The most powerful part of the nurturing process is what I call the "engagement spiral" - a way of deepening the relationship through increasingly meaningful interactions.

The engagement spiral visualizes how relationships deepen over time through increasingly meaningful interactions:

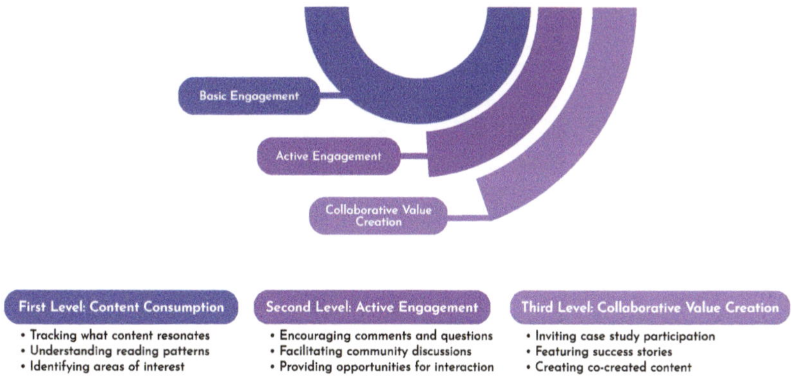

This spiral visualization shows the natural progression from basic content consumption through active engagement to collaborative value creation. The metrics at each level demonstrate how engagement typically narrows but deepens as relationships progress, with each level requiring more commitment but delivering greater value.

First Level: Content Consumption

- Tracking what content resonates
- Understanding reading patterns
- dentifying areas of interest

Second Level: Active Engagement

- Encouraging comments and questions
- Facilitating community discussions
- Providing opportunities for interaction

Third Level: Collaborative Value Creation

- Inviting case study participation
- Featuring success stories
- Creating co-created content

For example, one reader went from consuming blog posts to participating in webinars, then sharing their implementation story, and finally becoming a case study that helped others in their journey. This natural progression built a strong relationship long before they became a consulting client.

The Personalization Framework

One of the most powerful insights I've gained is that effective nurturing requires systematic personalization. Here's the framework I developed:

1. Entry Point Personalization Understanding how someone finds you reveals their initial interests. Someone who discovers you through a technical article has different needs than someone who finds you through a strategic piece.

2. Behavioral Personalization Tracking how people interact with your content reveals their evolving interests. When someone shifts from reading technical posts to leadership content, it often signals a career transition - a perfect time to adjust your nurturing approach.

3. Engagement Personalization Different people engage in different ways. Some prefer detailed written content, others respond better to video or interactive tools. By tracking these preferences, you can deliver content in the most effective format for each person.

Measuring Nurturing Effectiveness

The key to improving your nurturing efforts lies in measuring the right things. Through years of refining my approach, I've identified three critical dimensions of measurement that tell the complete story of your nurturing success.

First, we need to understand engagement depth - the degree to which people are truly connecting with your content and offerings. This goes far beyond simple page views or email opens. We need to see if readers are progressively diving deeper into your content ecosystem, moving naturally from blog posts to guides to workshops. Are they not just consuming your content, but finding it valuable enough to share with their networks? When I noticed that readers who engaged with at least three different content types were five times more likely to become clients, it completely changed how we structured our content journey.

The second dimension I track closely is relationship velocity - the pace at which relationships develop with your audience. This isn't about pushing people faster through a funnel; it's about understanding the natural rhythm of relationship building in your market. By analyzing thousands of customer journeys, we can identify common stalling points where people need additional support or information. More importantly, we can spot the triggers that tend to accelerate relationship development. In my practice, I discovered that participation in live webinars often served as a crucial acceleration point, prompting us to make them a more central part of our nurturing strategy.

Finally, and perhaps most crucially, we need to measure value realization - the actual results people achieve from engaging with your content and implementing your insights. This is where the rubber meets the road. Are people taking action on what they learn? What concrete results are they achieving? How are they sharing these successes with others? When we found that clients who actively shared their implementation stories were more likely to achieve better results, we built sharing mechanisms directly into our program structure.

Together, these three dimensions of measurement provide a comprehensive view of your nurturing effectiveness, allowing you to refine and improve your approach continuously while staying focused on what truly matters - helping your audience achieve real results.

With a clear understanding of our audience and a solid value delivery system in place, we can now bring everything together into a practical execution framework. To make this concrete, let's look at how these principles apply in a real-world scenario.

VI. Execution Framework: Bringing It All Together

Now that we've explored the principles of digital sales, value delivery, and audience nurturing, let's see how these concepts can be applied in practice. To make this concrete, I'll share how we're planning to implement these principles in ZapZap (tryzapzap.com), a comprehensive business management platform currently under development that will integrate strategic planning with execution.

This example is particularly relevant because it demonstrates how to apply our digital sales framework to a SaaS product from its inception - something many of you are likely building. While our previous examples focused on consulting services, let's explore how these principles are being adapted for a product in development.

Understanding the Value Journey

Our digital sales strategy for ZapZap is being built around a clear understanding of how businesses evolve in their journey toward better management and execution. The platform will bring together business dashboards for real-time insights, strategic planning tools for vision and goal-setting, operational roadmaps for turning strategy into action, and team Kanbans for day-to-day execution. However, rather than promoting all these features at once, we're designing our approach to meet businesses where they are in their journey.

Through our research and customer interviews during the platform's development phase, we've identified a common progression in management maturity. Companies typically start at the awareness stage, realizing they need better visibility into their operations. They then move into the organization stage, where they begin formalizing their strategic planning processes. This naturally leads to the implementation stage, where they're ready to create operational roadmaps. Finally, they reach the integration stage, seeking to connect their strategy with daily execution.

Building the Value Delivery System

Understanding this progression is shaping how we're structuring our value delivery system. At the entry level, we're developing a free Business Health Assessment tool that will help companies identify their management gaps. This tool will provide immediate value without requiring any commitment, while naturally demonstrating the need for more comprehensive solutions.

We're also developing a Management Insights Hub that will serve as our educational layer. Through detailed guides on strategic planning, case studies of successful business transformations, and best practices for operational execution, we'll demonstrate our expertise while showing how ZapZap will solve specific challenges. Each piece of content is being crafted to provide standalone value while naturally highlighting the benefits of our platform.

To bridge the gap between education and implementation, we're creating a suite of practical tools. Our strategic planning templates, roadmap frameworks, and team collaboration guides will provide immediate utility while showcasing the benefits of full platform integration. When users experience value from these free tools, the transition to the full platform will become a natural next step.

The Planned Sales Funnel

Our digital sales funnel will begin with content that addresses common business challenges. Articles like "Why Most Strategic Plans Fail" and "The Missing Link Between Strategy and Execution" will attract leaders grappling with these issues. This content will establish our expertise while introducing the concepts behind our solution.

The engagement phase will center around interactive tools providing immediate value. Our Business Management Assessment, Strategy Template Generator, and Team Collaboration Analyzer will give potential users tangible insights they can apply immediately. These tools will also help us understand where each business is in their management journey.

Our nurture phase will provide segmented education based on business size and needs. Startups will receive guidance on establishing foundational processes, growing companies will learn about scaling and optimization, and enterprise clients will explore complex integration scenarios. This segmented approach will ensure every business receives relevant, actionable insights.

The conversion phase will offer multiple entry points based on readiness. Some companies will start with a free trial of our basic dashboards, others will begin with department-specific pilots, and enterprise clients will often engage through proof of concept implementations. This flexibility will allow each organization to adopt ZapZap in a way that aligns with their needs and comfort level.

Implementation Roadmap

Our planned implementation timeline spans three months of carefully orchestrated activities.

Here's a visual roadmap of the key activities and milestones across the three-month implementation:

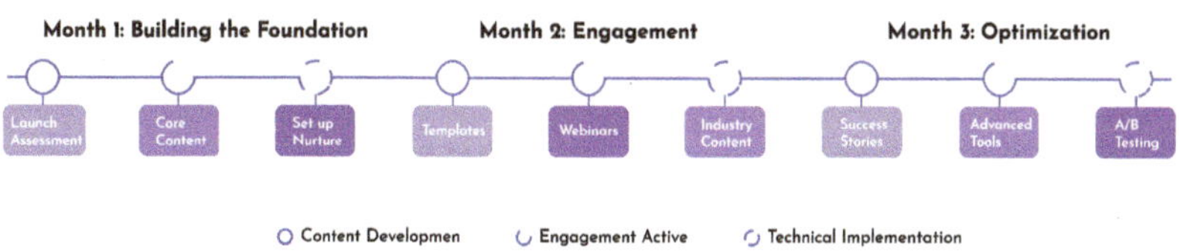

This timeline highlights the critical activities in each phase, color-coded by type. Notice how the foundation phase focuses on basic infrastructure, the engagement phase introduces more interactive elements, and the optimization phase focuses on refinement and scaling. The milestone markers indicate key checkpoints where progress should be evaluated before moving forward.

Month 1: Building the Foundation

- Launch the Business Health Assessment tool
- Create core educational content
- Set up nurture sequences
- Implement conversion tracking

Month 2: Deepening Engagement

- Release management templates
- Begin webinar series
- Launch industry-specific content
- Implement lead scoring

Month 3: Optimization

- Share early customer success stories
- Launch advanced calculators
- Begin A/B testing program
- Refine nurture sequences

As we develop and implement this framework, we recognize that one element becomes increasingly critical: trust. In the digital age, trust isn't just a nice-to-have - it's the foundation upon which all successful digital sales are built.

By sharing our implementation plans for ZapZap openly, we're not just describing a theoretical framework - we're inviting you to follow along as we put these principles into practice. You can follow our progress at tryzapzap.com and learn from both our successes and challenges as we build this platform using the very principles outlined in this book.

VII. Building Trust and Scaling Relationships

In the SaaS world, trust isn't just about credibility - it's about demonstrating consistent value and reliability. In developing ZapZap, we recognize that the traditional hard sell approach of showcasing features and pushing for immediate signups often backfires. That's why we're developing a trust-building framework specifically designed for digital products.

The Value-First Foundation

At the foundation of our planned trust-building approach lies what we call the "value-first demonstration." Rather than just describing ZapZap's Business Dashboards, we'll offer a free Business Health Assessment tool that provides immediate insights. This will show potential users the kind of value they can expect from the full platform, without asking for any commitment in return. Based on our research and experience with similar tools, we expect companies using our assessment tool will be significantly more likely to become paid users compared to those who only see feature demonstrations.

Educational Leadership

Educational leadership forms the second pillar of our trust-building strategy. Instead of pushing features, we'll focus on educating about business management best practices.

We're developing comprehensive guides on strategic planning implementation, preparing real-world case studies that will demonstrate successful business transformations. Our content library will include practical templates, frameworks, and industry benchmarks. This approach will position us not just as a software provider, but as a trusted advisor in business management.

Community Building

Community building will be the third crucial element in our trust framework. We're planning to create vibrant spaces where users can share experiences and learn from each other. Starting with a simple user forum, we envision evolving into a dynamic ecosystem of peer learning. Business leaders will be able to share their implementation stories, discuss industry-specific challenges, and celebrate successes together. Regular virtual meetups will become must-attend events where users not only learn new strategies but build valuable connections with peers facing similar challenges.

Multi-Platform Engagement

Our social media presence will reflect this trust-building approach across different platforms:

- **LinkedIn:** In-depth strategic insights and analysis, sparking meaningful discussions among business leaders
- **Twitter:** Quick management tips and celebration of user achievements
- **Instagram:** A window into our product development process and company culture, helping users connect with the humans behind the platform

- **Weekly expert sessions:** Tackling complex business challenges with industry experts

Personalized User Journey

The email strategy we're designing focuses on driving meaningful product adoption through personalized journeys. When a new user joins ZapZap, they won't be bombarded with feature tutorials. Instead, we'll guide them through a carefully crafted journey:

Day 1: Simple setup guide guaranteeing quick wins Day 3: First dashboard creation Week 1: Introduction to team collaboration features Week 2: Introduction to strategic planning capabilities

Feature Adoption Strategy

Our feature adoption sequences will follow a behavior-driven philosophy:

- Basic dashboard mastery triggers introduction to advanced analytics
- Successful project tracking leads to strategic objective linking
- Each step will build naturally on user progress, not arbitrary timeframes

Celebrating Success

Success celebration will be a core part of the user journey. We plan to recognize achievements both big and small:

- Completing first strategic plan
- Achieving team milestones
- Demonstrating positive ROI
- Sharing success stories to inspire other users

The Vision for Trust-Building

This comprehensive approach to trust-building is central to how we envision users engaging with ZapZap. We're not just building software - we're creating a partnership platform for businesses on their journey to better management and execution. Based on similar implementations, we expect this approach to drive strong user retention, high referral rates, and most importantly, help our users achieve their business objectives more consistently.

You can follow our progress in implementing these trust-building strategies at tryzapzap.com. As we develop and launch each component, we'll be documenting our learnings and sharing insights with our community. This transparency in our own building process is itself a demonstration of our commitment to trust-based relationships with our users.

VIII. Scaling Through International Markets

The most powerful aspect of digital sales that many startups overlook is its incredible potential for international expansion. I discovered this almost by accident during my journey with the ADAPT Methodology. After years of building a substantial library of content in English, I stumbled upon a remarkable opportunity when I moved to Saudi Arabia.

Let me share how this discovery transformed my approach to scaling across markets.

The Power of Content Localization

My journey into international markets began with a simple realization: the content that had taken years to create in English represented an invaluable asset that could be leveraged in other markets. I had hundreds of blog posts, each tested and proven to attract and engage readers interested in Agile methodologies. This wasn't just content - it was a blueprint for market entry.

When I moved to Saudi Arabia, I started experimenting with translating some of our most successful English content into Arabic. The results were astounding. Keywords that we could never hope to rank for in the highly competitive English-language market suddenly put us at the top of Arabic Google searches. Within months, Saudi Arabia became our third most visited country. The key wasn't just translation - it was understanding that less competition in the Arabic market meant our high-quality content could have an even bigger impact.

This success wasn't a one-off. I had previously seen similar results in the German market, and being Portuguese, I naturally expanded into Portugal as well. Each new market followed the same pattern: take proven content, adapt it thoughtfully for the local audience, and watch the leads flow in.

A Simple Path to International Growth

The beauty of this approach lies in its simplicity. You don't need to reinvent your marketing strategy for each country. Instead, start with what you know works. In my case, I knew exactly which English posts generated the most engagement and leads. These became our priority for translation and localization.

But success isn't just about translating content. The real magic happens when you combine localized content with local talent. After establishing a strong flow of Arabic-language leads, the next step was bringing on business development managers who understood the local market. They could take our proven follow-up processes and adapt them to local business customs and expectations.

This two-step approach - first content, then local sales support - creates a powerful entry mechanism into new markets. It's far more efficient than trying to build a presence from scratch in each country. You're essentially taking a proven playbook and adapting it rather than starting over each time.

The Economics of International Expansion

What makes this approach particularly powerful is its favorable economics. The hard work of creating the original content - figuring out what topics resonate, what questions to answer, what problems to solve - has already been done. The cost of translation and localization is relatively small compared to the original content creation cost, yet the potential return is just as large, sometimes larger in less competitive markets.

Consider this: a blog post that took days to research, write, and refine in English might take only hours to adapt for a new market. Yet in that new market, it could generate just as many leads as the original. The return on investment can be extraordinary, especially when you target markets where competition for your keywords is less fierce.

Building for Long-Term Success

The key to making this work long-term is maintaining quality through the localization process. This isn't about running content through Google Translate and hoping for the best. It's about thoughtful adaptation that preserves the value of the original while making it culturally relevant to the new audience.

Success also requires patience and consistency. When we entered the Saudi market, we didn't just translate a few posts and hope for the best. We committed to a steady stream of localized content, building our Arabic library just as we had built our English one. This consistent effort signals to both search engines and potential customers that you're serious about serving their market.

This approach to international expansion has transformed how I think about scaling startups. It's not just about growing in your home market - it's about leveraging your proven content and processes to build a truly global presence. The digital nature of modern sales makes this more achievable than ever before.

Looking Forward

As you build your digital sales engine, keep this international potential in mind from the start. Document what works in your primary market. Track which content generates the most engagement and leads. This information becomes invaluable when you're ready to expand internationally.

Remember, the goal isn't to be everywhere at once. Start with markets where you have some natural advantage - whether that's language capability, cultural understanding, or simply less competition. Success in one new market will give you both the resources and the template for expansion into others.

In today's interconnected world, the ability to scale across markets isn't just an opportunity - it's increasingly a necessity for startups aiming for significant growth. The beauty of digital sales is that it gives you the tools to do this efficiently and effectively, turning local success into global opportunity.

Blueprint Summary

To scale successfully in today's digital landscape, startups must transform their traditional sales approach into a systematic digital engine. Here are the five key elements that make this possible:

1. **Digital Sales Mindset & Engine**
   - Transform from traditional interruption-based selling to value-driven attraction
   - Build systematic content creation and distribution processes
   - Create compound content that generates value over time
   - Implement efficient automation while maintaining human connection
   - Focus on relationship building rather than transactions
2. **Value Delivery System**
   - Develop four layers: Discovery, Educational, Implementation, and Transformational value

- Create value bridges between different stages of customer journey
- Build comprehensive tools and resources that solve immediate problems
- Implement value-first approach before asking for purchase
- Measure and optimize value delivery effectiveness

3. **Audience Understanding & Nurturing**
   - Analyze audience at surface, middle, and deep levels
   - Create personalized welcome and nurturing sequences
   - Build engagement spirals for deepening relationships
   - Implement behavioral-based segmentation
   - Track engagement depth, relationship velocity, and value realization
4. **Trust-Building Framework**
   - Demonstrate value before requesting commitment
   - Provide educational leadership in your domain
   - Build community around shared challenges
   - Create personalized user journeys
   - Celebrate customer successes and milestones
5. **International Market Scaling**
   - Leverage existing content for new market entry

- Localize proven content for different languages
- Combine content strategy with local sales talent
- Target underserved markets for maximum impact
- Maintain consistent quality across markets

Conclusion

The journey to effective digital sales transcends individual tactics or tools - it requires building a comprehensive system that delivers consistent value while scaling personal relationships. Success comes from fundamentally shifting how we think about sales, moving from traditional transaction-focused approaches to building value-driven relationships at scale.

What makes this approach particularly powerful is its scalability across markets and cultures. By building a solid content foundation and value delivery system in your primary market, you create assets that can be leveraged globally. Through thoughtful localization and market adaptation, you can create multiple growth engines running in parallel, each building on your core framework while resonating with local audiences.

The key to long-term success lies in maintaining the delicate balance between automation and personalization. While systems and processes enable scale, the human element remains crucial. Your digital sales engine should be treated as a product in itself - something that requires constant refinement and optimization based on user feedback and changing market conditions.

Remember, in the digital age, your sales process is often your customers' first experience with your brand. By implementing these five key elements - mindset transformation, value delivery, audience nurturing, trust building, and international scaling - you create a system that not only drives growth but builds lasting relationships with your users across global markets.

The future belongs to companies that can master this balance between scale and personalization, between automation and human connection, between global reach and local relevance. Your digital sales engine is the key to unlocking this future.

Put These Ideas Into Action

Get your free unicorn Blueprint Field Guide with templates & worksheets

Scan the QR code or visit the URL below to access your resources
https://scaleupmethodology.com/the-unicorn-blueprint-fieldguide/

Chapter No. 2

CONTINUOUS DELIVERY: Unleash Engineering Excellence

I. The Midnight Deploy

The night was eerily quiet at Nokia's headquarters as I sat at my desk, the only engineer still present on that cold September evening in 2005. As a junior software engineer, I often worked late, but this night was different. I was about to witness something that would shape my entire understanding of software development.

At precisely midnight, our build system sprang to life. What unfolded before me seemed like pure magic - a perfectly choreographed symphony of automation. Code from over 3,000 engineers across different time zones began flowing into our systems. Each contribution was automatically compiled, systematically deployed to hundreds of test phones, and subjected to rigorous automated testing sequences. By morning, a new version of Nokia's operating system would be ready for validation.

This wasn't just an impressive technical feat; it was a glimpse into the future of software development. A future where releases weren't dreaded events but routine occurrences, where quality was built into the process rather than tacked on at the end, and where businesses could respond to market demands at the speed of thought.

Let me illustrate this midnight automation symphony that unfolded before me at Nokia. This system, handling code from over 3,000 engineers worldwide, represented one of the most sophisticated automated build processes of its time.

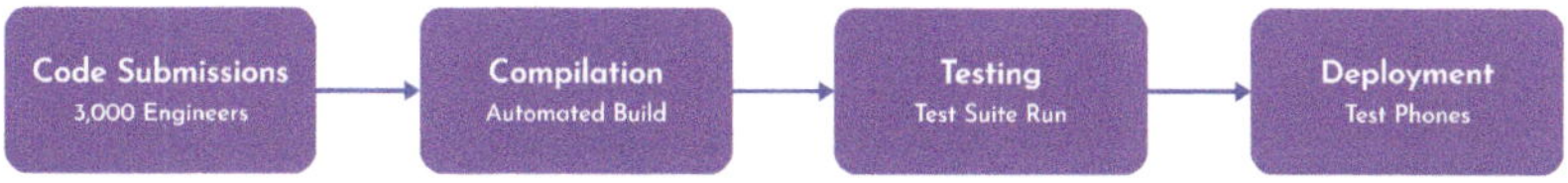

As shown in the visualization, the process began at midnight with code submissions flowing in from different time zones. The system then moved through four critical stages: code collection, automated compilation, systematic testing, and finally deployment to hundreds of test phones. Notice how each stage built upon the previous one, creating a seamless flow that transformed raw code into a testable operating system by morning. This level of automation in 2005 demonstrated what was possible with proper tooling and processes – a lesson that remains relevant for today's startups.

II. The State of Continuous Delivery

Fast forward to 2024, and I find myself in countless meetings with startup founders and CTOs who view Continuous Delivery as a luxury they can't afford. "We're too small," they say. "It's too complex for our team." Each time I hear these words, I'm transported back to that night at Nokia. If we could orchestrate automated deployments with thousands of engineers and millions of lines of code in 2005, surely today's startups can achieve the same with modern tools and smaller codebases.

The reality is stark: companies that resist adopting Continuous Delivery often pay a heavy price. I witnessed this firsthand with a startup that insisted their four releases per year were "good enough." Every release required three weeks of company-wide testing, effectively paralyzing the entire organization. Their resistance to change culminated in a catastrophic incident that cost them $5 million in lost revenue over just three months. Their codebase had become so tangled that fixing one bug inevitably introduced two more.

Yet the cost of delay extends far beyond immediate financial losses. I've seen promising startups lose market opportunities because they couldn't ship features fast enough. I've watched talented developers leave organizations out of frustration with slow, manual deployment processes. Most painfully, I've observed customers abandon products due to slow bug fixes and infrequent updates.

The truth is, Continuous Delivery isn't just about deploying code faster - it's about building a sustainable, scalable foundation for your startup's growth. When implemented properly, it transforms not just your deployment process, but your entire approach to software development. Teams become more confident, customers more satisfied, and businesses more agile.

As we explore the principles and practices of Continuous Delivery in this chapter, remember that this isn't just about implementing tools or following a process. It's about creating a technical foundation that enables your startup to move fast without breaking things. It's about building a machine that can reliably and consistently deliver value to your customers.

Let's begin by understanding the core pillars that make Continuous Delivery possible, and how you can implement them in your organization, regardless of your size or current technical maturity.

II. The Five Pillars of Continuous Delivery Success

The journey to Continuous Delivery excellence is built upon five fundamental pillars. Like the columns of an ancient temple, each pillar plays a crucial role in supporting the whole structure. Through my years of consulting with startups and enterprises alike, I've seen organizations succeed when they strengthen these pillars together, and fail when they neglect even one. Let's explore each pillar and understand how they work together to create a robust delivery system.

Before we dive into each component, let's visualize how these five fundamental pillars work together to support successful Continuous Delivery. Like a temple's architecture, each pillar plays a crucial and complementary role.

THE FIVE PILLARS OF CONTINUOUS DELIVERY

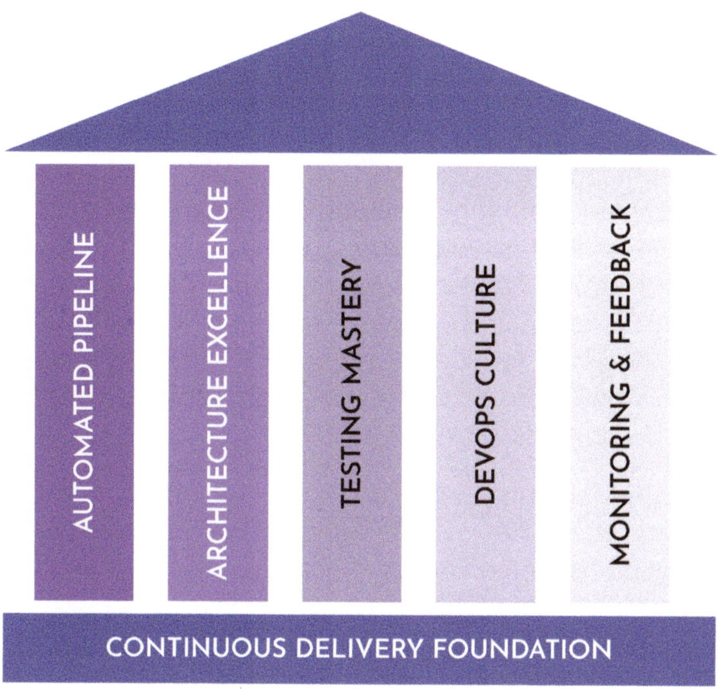

Looking at the diagram, you'll notice how each pillar – Automated Pipeline, Architecture Excellence, Testing Mastery, DevOps Culture, and Monitoring & Feedback – supports the overall structure. The foundation represents your organization's commitment to Continuous Delivery, while each pillar contributes equally to the system's stability.

The proportions are intentional – weakening any single pillar puts the entire structure at risk. This interdependence is key to understanding why successful Continuous Delivery requires attention to all five areas.

A. The Automated Pipeline: Building Your Delivery Machine

I often tell startup founders that a manual deployment process is like trying to drive a car by getting out and pushing it - you'll get there eventually, but it's not a sustainable way to travel. The automated pipeline is your engine, transforming raw code into running software without human intervention.

The "Kitten Builds" story from 2012 perfectly illustrates this point. I was working with a company that was deeply resistant to automation. Despite our best efforts to convince management of its value, we couldn't break through - until we tried something unconventional. The company had three massive screens in their lobby, each about 3x3 meters. We hatched a plan to display our build results there, showing huge crying kittens when the build failed and dancing kittens when it succeeded.

While management shut down our experiment after just one day, that brief display sparked crucial conversations throughout the organization. People who had never thought about the build process before suddenly became invested in its success. Two years later, I learned the company had fully embraced automation and was deploying multiple times daily - a process that previously took weeks.

The success of an automated pipeline rests on three key components working in harmony. First, continuous integration ensures that code changes are frequently merged and tested, preventing the dreaded "integration hell" that plagues manual processes. Second, automated testing provides confidence that changes haven't broken existing functionality. Finally, deployment automation ensures that validated code can be reliably deployed to any environment at the push of a button.

B. Architecture Excellence: Designing for Change

"Your architecture is either enabling your success or ensuring your failure." These words from a mentor early in my career have proven true time and time again. I witnessed this firsthand with a Berlin-based startup that had hit a wall with their monolithic application. Every deployment had become a nerve-wracking event that could take days, and each change carried the risk of bringing down the entire system.

Their transformation began with a crucial realization: architecture isn't just about technology choices - it's about enabling teams to work effectively. The team embarked on a journey to gradually break their monolith into microservices, starting with the most frequently changing components. They didn't try to do everything at once; instead, they followed a methodical approach:

First, they identified natural service boundaries based on business domains. Then, they began building new features as separate services while gradually extracting existing functionality. Throughout this process, they maintained backward compatibility to ensure business continuity. The results were transformative: deployment times dropped from days to minutes, team productivity increased by 40%, and system reliability improved significantly.

C. Testing Mastery: Building Confidence Through Verification

One of my most memorable consulting experiences was with a fintech startup that had an unusual problem: they were testing too much, but paradoxically, not testing effectively. Every release required three weeks of manual testing, yet critical bugs still slipped through to production. Their approach to testing was like trying to ensure a car is safe by having a hundred people walk around it once, rather than having expert mechanics systematically check each component.

We introduced them to the testing pyramid concept, but not as a theoretical framework - we made it tangible. We started with unit tests as the foundation, focusing on quick, reliable feedback for developers. Integration tests formed the middle layer, verifying that components worked together correctly. End-to-end tests crowned the pyramid, validating complete user journeys but in smaller, more focused numbers.

The testing pyramid is more than just a concept – it's a strategic approach to balancing different types of tests in your automation suite. Let's examine this crucial model in detail.

The Testing Pyramid

A Strategic Approach to Test Automation

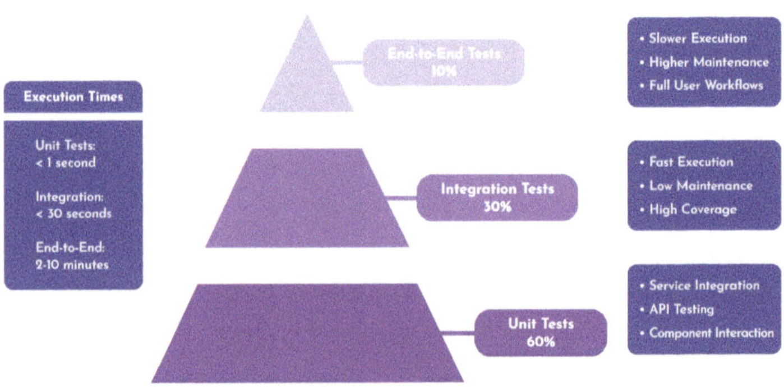

Unit tests form the foundation of the testing strategy with higher coverage and faster execution time

Notice how the pyramid's structure reflects both the quantity and scope of each testing type. At the base, unit tests form the foundation, comprising about 60% of your test suite. These fast, focused tests provide immediate feedback to developers. The middle layer of integration tests (30%) verifies component interactions, while the top layer of end-to-end tests (10%) validates complete user journeys. This proportion ensures both comprehensive coverage and efficient test execution. The narrowing towards the top reflects how tests become slower and more complex as they expand in scope.

The real breakthrough came when we implemented "Testing Tuesday" - a weekly event where the entire company participated in exploratory testing. This wasn't your typical bug hunt; it was a collaborative learning experience. Marketing team members discovered usability issues that developers had never considered. Customer support staff identified edge cases based on their experience with user problems. Even the CEO's participation led to insights about business-critical workflows that weren't adequately tested.

The results spoke for themselves: a 60% reduction in post-release incidents and significantly improved customer satisfaction scores. But more importantly, testing transformed from a dreaded checkpoint into a collaborative activity that brought the entire organization together.

D. DevOps Culture: Breaking Down the Walls

The importance of culture in Continuous Delivery became crystal clear to me through an experience with a Lisbon-based fintech startup. On paper, they had all the right tools and processes, yet deployments still failed regularly. The root cause? A deep divide between their development and operations teams.

It reminded me of a restaurant where the chefs and servers never communicate - the food might be excellent, and the service might be great, but if they're not coordinating, the customer experience suffers. In this startup's case, developers would "throw code over the wall" to operations, who would then struggle to deploy it without crucial context about the changes.

Their transformation began with a simple but powerful change: creating cross-functional teams responsible for services from development through production. This wasn't just an organizational change; it was a mindset shift. Developers started thinking about operational requirements while coding. Operations teams began participating in design decisions. When issues arose, there was no finger-pointing - just collaborative problem-solving.

The impact was dramatic. Their deployment success rate soared from 65% to 98%. Mean Time To Recovery (MTTR) dropped by 70%. Most tellingly, team satisfaction scores doubled as the previous adversarial relationship transformed into a partnership.

E. Monitoring & Feedback: The Eyes and Ears of Your System

Let me share a story about a Munich-based e-commerce platform that learned this lesson the hard way. Like many companies, they only discovered problems when customers complained. Their monitoring strategy, if you could call it that, was essentially waiting for something to break and then scrambling to fix it.

Everything changed during their Black Friday sale when their system crashed under unexpected load. The post-mortem revealed that warning signs had been present for weeks - they just didn't have the tools to see them. This crisis became their catalyst for transformation.

They implemented comprehensive monitoring that went beyond basic uptime checks. Technical metrics tracked system performance and resource utilization. Business metrics monitored user engagement and feature adoption. Most importantly, they set up early warning systems that could predict potential issues before they impacted customers.

The transformation was remarkable. Instead of discovering problems through customer complaints, they began catching and fixing issues before users noticed them. System reliability improved to 99.99% uptime during peak seasons. When issues did occur, root cause identification time dropped from hours to minutes. Perhaps most impressively, their operational costs decreased by 40% despite handling more traffic than ever before.

The lesson here isn't just about having more monitoring tools - it's about creating a feedback loop that drives continuous improvement. Every incident became a learning opportunity. Every metric told a story. Every alert helped them understand their system better.

III. Building Your Continuous Delivery Machine

Having explored the foundational pillars, let's turn to the practical aspects of building your Continuous Delivery machine. I often tell teams that implementing Continuous Delivery is like constructing a factory - you need the right tools, a clear implementation strategy, and most importantly, skilled people who understand how to use both.

A. The Technology Stack: Choosing Your Tools Wisely

I'll never forget a conversation with a startup CTO who had spent six months evaluating different CI/CD tools, yet hadn't deployed a single automated pipeline. "We need to choose the perfect tool," he insisted. I reminded him that a master chef can create amazing dishes with basic tools, while an amateur will struggle even with the finest equipment.

The technology stack for Continuous Delivery isn't about having the latest, trendiest tools - it's about having the right tools for your context. Let me share how we helped this CTO break through analysis paralysis and build a working system.

We started with version control - Git, in this case - but it wasn't just about storing code. We implemented thoughtful branching strategies and code review workflows that matched their team's size and capabilities. Rather than copying industry giants' complex processes, we created simple, effective workflows that their team could actually follow.

For CI/CD platforms, we evaluated options based on their specific needs. Jenkins offered the flexibility they needed for their unique build requirements. While competitors had flashier interfaces, Jenkins' extensive plugin ecosystem and customization capabilities made it the right choice for their context. The key was not the tool itself, but how we used it to automate their specific workflows.

Infrastructure tools proved particularly challenging. The team was initially attracted to Kubernetes because "everyone is using it," but their simple application didn't require such complexity. Instead, we started with basic infrastructure as code using Terraform, automating their AWS infrastructure in a way that matched their current needs while leaving room for growth.

B. Implementation Strategy: The Art of Starting Small

One of my most successful projects began with a failure. A rapidly growing startup had attempted to implement full

Continuous Delivery all at once. Three months in, they had nothing to show for it except frustrated teams and skeptical stakeholders. When they brought me in, I suggested a different approach: start small, but start now.

We began with what I call "quick wins" - high-impact, low-effort improvements that could demonstrate value quickly. The first week, we simply automated their build process, reducing build times from 45 minutes to 10 minutes. This single improvement saved each developer nearly an hour per day and built immediate credibility for our broader initiatives.

Over the next three months, we systematically expanded our automation. Each improvement was small, but they compounded powerfully. By month two, we had automated unit tests running on every commit. By month three, we had automated deployments to staging environments. The key was that each step delivered tangible value and built momentum for the next phase.

Our implementation roadmap looked like this:

Phase 1 focused on the basics - continuous integration, automated testing, and deployment scripts. We weren't aiming for perfection; we just needed to prove that automation could work in their environment.

Phase 2 expanded our scope to include automated deployments to staging, more comprehensive testing, and basic monitoring. This was where teams started to feel the full benefits of their earlier investments.

Phase 3 brought everything together with production automation, advanced testing strategies, and comprehensive monitoring. By this point, teams were fully bought in because they'd experienced the benefits firsthand.

Implementing Continuous Delivery is a journey that requires

careful planning and progressive improvements. Let's map out a realistic 90-day implementation timeline that has proven successful across multiple organizations.

90-Day Continuous Delivery Implementation Plan

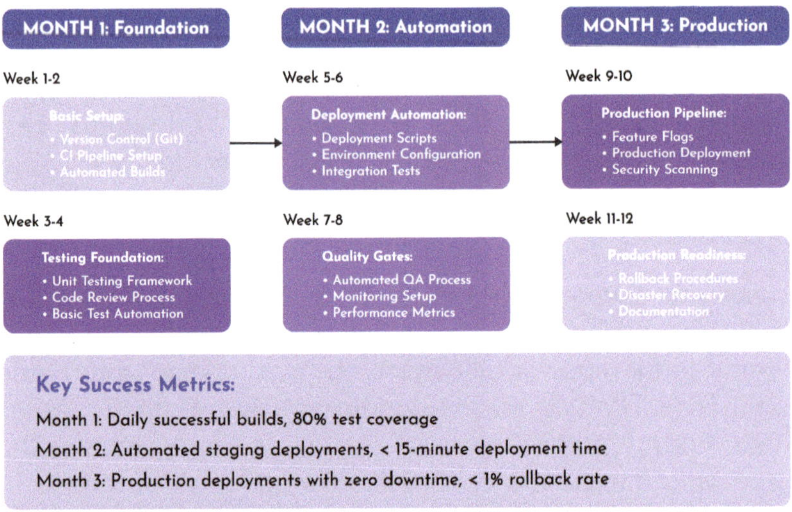

This timeline breaks down the journey into three critical phases. The foundation phase (Days 1-30) focuses on establishing basic automation and version control – notice how these fundamental elements enable all future improvements. The automation phase (Days 31-60) builds upon this foundation with more sophisticated testing and deployment capabilities.

Finally, the production phase (Days 61-90) introduces advanced features like feature flags and comprehensive monitoring. Each phase has clear deliverables and success metrics, allowing teams to track their progress effectively.

C. The Human Element: Your Most Critical Component

Perhaps the most valuable lesson I've learned about Continuous Delivery came from an unexpected source - a resistant senior developer who later became one of our strongest advocates. His journey taught me that technical excellence alone isn't enough; you need to bring people along on the journey.

This senior developer, let's call him Marcus, had been with the company for eight years. "We've always done it this way," he would say when we suggested automating deployments. His resistance wasn't about technology - it was about pride in the craftsmanship of his manual deployment process. The turning point came when we reframed automation not as a replacement for his expertise, but as a tool to amplify it.

We discovered that successful Continuous Delivery transformations aren't just about training people on tools - they're about helping people understand their evolving role in a more automated world. Here's how we've learned to approach the human element:

First, we focus on skill development, but not in the way most organizations do. Rather than generic tool training, we create learning paths tailored to each team member's current expertise and future aspirations. For Marcus, this meant exploring how his deep system knowledge could help design more resilient automated processes. For junior developers, it meant understanding how automation could help them learn from senior team members' expertise.

Change management comes next, but it's not about following a textbook approach. It's about understanding and addressing the real human concerns behind resistance to change. When a QA team worried that test automation would make their roles obsolete, we showed them how automation of routine tests would free them to do more interesting exploratory testing. When operations teams feared losing control, we demonstrated how automation would give them more visibility and control, not less.

The most successful transformations happen when teams reorganize around the flow of value to customers. I remember working with a company that traditionally had separate development, QA, and operations teams. Each team was highly skilled, but their separation created delays and misunderstandings. We helped them create cross-functional teams where developers, QA engineers, and operations specialists worked together from the start of each feature.

The results were remarkable. Not only did delivery speed increase, but team satisfaction improved dramatically. Developers gained a deeper understanding of operational concerns. QA engineers could influence design decisions earlier in the process. Operations specialists could provide infrastructure insights during initial planning rather than discovering problems during deployment.

Support systems proved crucial for sustaining these changes. We established clear escalation paths so teams knew how to get help when needed. Knowledge sharing became part of the daily routine through tech talks and pair programming sessions. Mentoring programs paired experienced automation engineers with those just starting their journey.

Perhaps most importantly, we created space for experimentation and learning. Regular retrospectives allowed teams to reflect on what was working and what wasn't. When things went wrong - and they occasionally did - we focused on learning rather than blame. Each incident became an opportunity to improve our processes and automation.

I'll never forget the day Marcus, our once-resistant senior developer, came to me with an idea for automating a particularly complex deployment scenario. "I used to think automation would make my job less important," he said, "but now I see it lets me focus on the interesting problems." That's when I knew our transformation had truly succeeded - when the team started seeing Continuous Delivery not as something imposed on them, but as a tool that empowered them to do their best work.

The human element of Continuous Delivery isn't just about managing change or training people on new tools. It's about creating an environment where people can grow, learn, and do their best work. When you get this right, the technical challenges of Continuous Delivery become much easier to solve because you have an engaged, motivated team working together toward a common goal.

IV. Advanced Continuous Delivery Beyond the Basics

Once you've mastered the fundamentals of Continuous Delivery, a whole new world of possibilities opens up. This is where things get really interesting - and where I've seen companies truly differentiate themselves from their competitors. Let me share some stories that illustrate these advanced practices in action.

A. Production Testing Strategies: Testing in the Real World

The most valuable lesson about production testing I ever learned came from a catastrophic launch at a streaming service. They had spent months testing their new recommendation engine in staging environments, yet within hours of launching to production, the system began recommending horror movies to children's accounts. Their staging tests had looked perfect, but they hadn't accounted for the complexity of real-world user behavior.

This incident led us to develop a more sophisticated approach to production testing. We implemented canary releases, initially rolling out changes to just 1% of users. Think of it as dipping your toe in the water before diving in. When we detected any issues - from performance degradation to unusual user behavior - we could quickly roll back with minimal impact.

A/B testing became another powerful tool in our arsenal. Rather than debating whether a new feature would work better than an existing one, we could test both versions simultaneously with real users. One e-commerce client discovered that a checkout flow they were certain would increase conversions actually reduced them by 15% - information they never would have gotten from staging environments alone.

Feature flags transformed how we managed releases. Instead of massive, risky deployments, we could ship code to production but keep it disabled until we were ready to activate it. When a major financial services company needed to roll out a new trading algorithm, they used feature flags to gradually enable it for different customer segments, carefully monitoring for any anomalies before expanding the rollout.

B. Scaling Continuous Delivery: Growing Without Breaking

The challenges of scaling Continuous Delivery became personal for me when I helped a rapidly growing startup expand from 5 to 50 development teams in just 18 months. What worked perfectly for one team became a bottleneck for ten teams, and what worked for ten teams nearly collapsed under the weight of fifty.

Multi-team coordination emerged as our biggest challenge. With teams spread across three continents, we needed more than just good tools - we needed a framework for collaboration. We established what we called "delivery guilds" - cross-team groups focused on specific aspects of the delivery pipeline. These guilds became the backbone of our scaling strategy, sharing best practices and solving common problems across teams.

Platform teams proved crucial to our success. Rather than having each team reinvent the wheel, we created a dedicated platform team that provided standardized deployment pipelines, monitoring solutions, and testing frameworks. This team didn't just build tools; they became internal consultants, helping other teams optimize their delivery processes.

Managing service boundaries became an art form. We learned that clear interfaces between services weren't just technical necessities - they were organizational tools that helped teams work independently while maintaining system cohesion. One team's morning deploy couldn't be allowed to break another team's service on the other side of the world.

C. Future Horizons: The Next Wave of Innovation

The future of Continuous Delivery is already taking shape in some fascinating ways. I recently worked with a team that's using AI to optimize their test selection, running only the tests most likely to catch issues based on the specific changes being deployed. Another client is experimenting with automated code review systems that not only catch potential bugs but suggest performance improvements.

But perhaps the most exciting developments are happening in non-software applications. A hardware manufacturer I advised is applying Continuous Delivery principles to their product development, using simulation-driven development and rapid prototyping to "deploy" hardware changes more frequently. A marketing team has adapted our deployment pipeline concepts to manage their campaign releases, complete with A/B testing and gradual rollouts.

V. The Blueprint for Success

After years of helping companies implement Continuous Delivery, I've learned that success rarely comes from following a rigid playbook. Instead, it comes from understanding where you are, where you need to go, and how to bridge that gap. Let me share how we turned around one of my most challenging projects - a company that had tried and failed three times to implement Continuous Delivery before we helped them succeed.

A. Assessment Framework:

When I first met with this company's leadership team, they were understandably skeptical. "We've tried this before," their CTO told me. "How will this time be different?" The difference, I explained, would start with how we assessed their current state.

Rather than jumping straight into tool selection or process changes, we spent two weeks doing a comprehensive assessment. We looked beyond the obvious technical metrics like deployment frequency and lead time. We sat with teams, observing their daily workflows. We tracked the life cycle of several features from inception to production. Most importantly, we identified the human and organizational factors that had derailed their previous attempts.

What emerged was a clear picture of their challenges. Their deployment frequency wasn't low because they lacked automation tools - they had plenty. It was low because teams didn't trust their test coverage. Their long lead times weren't primarily due to technical bottlenecks, but to handoff delays between siloed teams. Understanding these root causes was crucial to creating an effective transformation plan.

B. Implementation Roadmap: The Path Forward

With a clear understanding of their starting point, we created a roadmap that broke down the transformation into manageable chunks. Instead of trying to change everything at once, we focused on what I call "impact waves" - sequences of changes that build upon each other.

The first 30 days focused on quick wins that would build confidence. We started with their most painful problem: unreliable tests. Rather than rewriting their entire test suite, we identified and fixed the 20% of flaky tests that caused 80% of their test failures. This single improvement reduced their build pipeline failures by 60% and started rebuilding trust in their automated processes.

The next 90 days focused on building their foundation. We introduced infrastructure as code, but gradually. First for their development environments, then staging, and finally production. Teams could see the benefits at each step, making them eager for the next phase rather than resistant to it.

By the 180-day mark, we were implementing advanced practices like feature flags and canary releases. But here's the key: we weren't pushing these practices on reluctant teams. Instead, teams were pulling for these capabilities because they had experienced the benefits of earlier improvements and wanted more.

C. Measuring Success: Beyond the Basic Metrics

One of my favorite moments came during a review meeting six months into the transformation. The CTO who had been initially skeptical pulled up their metrics dashboard. Deployment frequency had increased from twice a month to several times per day. Lead time for changes had dropped from weeks to hours. But what really made him smile wasn't on that dashboard.

"For the first time in two years," he said, "we didn't have a single developer quit last quarter." Team morale had improved dramatically. Product managers reported better relationships with development teams. Customer satisfaction scores were trending upward.

This highlighted an important lesson about measuring success in Continuous Delivery transformations: while technical metrics are important, they're not the whole story. Yes, we tracked the standard metrics - deployment frequency, lead time, change failure rate, and time to recovery. But we also tracked metrics that mattered to different stakeholders:

For developers, we measured time spent waiting for builds and tests, frequency of after-hours support calls, and confidence in deployments. For product managers, we tracked time from idea to production and ability to respond to customer feedback. For executives, we monitored development costs, customer satisfaction, and team retention.

VI. Disaster Recovery and Business Continuity

The most important lessons about disaster recovery often come from experiencing disasters firsthand. I'll never forget the day a major retail client called me in panic mode. It was Black Friday, their biggest sales day of the year, and their deployment pipeline had completely frozen. Teams couldn't push critical fixes, the monitoring system was overwhelmed, and their revenue was dropping by millions with each passing hour.

The root cause? A simple misconfiguration in their continuous integration system had cascaded into a complete pipeline shutdown. But the real problem wasn't the technical glitch - it was that no one had a clear plan for what to do when the pipeline itself failed. This incident taught us a crucial lesson: in Continuous Delivery, your pipeline is now your production system, and it needs the same level of resilience planning as your customer-facing applications.

When pipeline failures occur, having a clear decision-making framework can mean the difference between minor disruption and major crisis. Let's examine a structured approach to disaster recovery.

Continuous Delivery Disaster Recovery Decision Tree

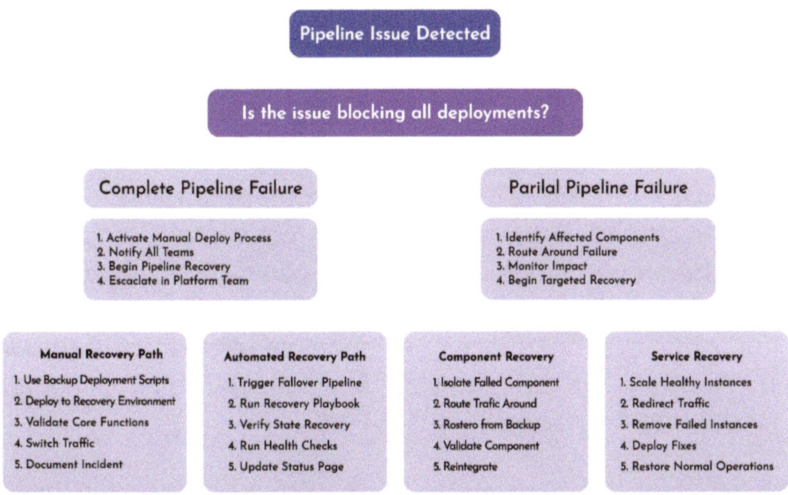

This decision tree guides teams through the critical first moments of a pipeline failure. Starting at the top with incident detection, teams first determine whether they're facing a complete or partial pipeline failure. Follow the left path for complete failures, which require immediate activation of manual deployment processes and full team notification.

The right path handles partial failures through component isolation and targeted recovery. Notice how each path includes specific actions and expected recovery times, providing clear guidance during high-stress situations.

A. When the Pipeline Breaks: Learning from Failure

The most dangerous assumption in Continuous Delivery is that your pipeline will always be available. A fintech startup learned this lesson the hard way. They had built what they thought was a bulletproof deployment system - multiple redundancies, automated failovers, the works. Then one day, their source code repository provider had a major outage. Suddenly, no one could push code, run tests, or deploy changes. Their "bulletproof" system had a single point of failure they hadn't considered.

This experience led us to develop what we call the "Pipeline Resilience Framework." Rather than relying on a single source control system, we established mirror repositories that synchronized continuously. We set up distributed build agents across different geographic regions, ensuring that if one datacenter went down, others could pick up the slack. Most importantly, we created and documented manual deployment procedures - not because we expected to use them often, but because we knew there would be times when automation wasn't an option.

B. The Art of Recovery: Beyond Backup Plans

Recovery isn't just about having backups - it's about having a clear, practiced plan for using them. A healthcare technology company learned this lesson the hard way when they had to roll back a critical deployment. They had backups of everything, but in the heat of the moment, no one knew exactly which backups to restore or in what order.

What should have been a 30-minute recovery turned into a 4-hour ordeal.

Working with their team, we developed a comprehensive recovery strategy that went beyond just creating backups. We established clear decision trees for different types of failures. Each scenario had a designated incident commander responsible for coordinating the response. Team members knew their roles and practiced them regularly. Perhaps most importantly, we created and regularly updated step-by-step recovery guides that were clear enough to follow even under extreme stress.

The key innovation was what we called “recovery checkpoints” - specific points in the recovery process where teams would stop and validate that everything was working as expected before proceeding. This prevented the all-too-common scenario where a rushed recovery actually makes things worse.

C. Building Resilient Systems

The best disaster recovery plan is the one you never need to use. This philosophy came to life through my work with a gaming company that took an unconventional approach to system resilience. Instead of waiting for failures to happen, they actively practiced what they called “pipeline chaos engineering” - deliberately introducing failures into their delivery system to test their recovery procedures.

Every Friday afternoon, a different team member would become the “chaos engineer” for the day. Their job? To break something in the pipeline in a controlled way. The twist? No one else knew what would break or when. One week, they might simulate a database failure. The next, they might take down the primary build agent. Through these exercises, they discovered countless weak points in their system that would have been catastrophic in a real emergency.

One particular exercise revealed a subtle but critical flaw in their setup. During a simulated network partition, they discovered that their backup build agents couldn't access certain private dependencies. In production, this would have meant a complete deployment freeze. By finding this in a controlled exercise, they were able to fix the issue before it became a real problem.

D. When Everything Falls Apart: The Human Side of Disaster Recovery

The most crucial element of disaster recovery isn't technical - it's human. I witnessed this firsthand during a severe incident at a financial services firm. Their lead developer, James, was brilliant with code but completely froze under the pressure of a production incident. With millions of dollars in transactions hanging in the balance, he knew the technical solution but couldn't execute under stress.

This experience taught us that psychological safety and clear communication are as important as technical procedures. We started incorporating stress management into our incident response training. Teams practiced communication under pressure using scenarios designed to be technically simple but emotionally challenging.

We introduced the concept of "incident partners" - two team members who would work together during crises, one handling the technical response while the other managed communication and coordination. This partnership approach proved invaluable during a later incident when a major deployment went wrong. While one partner worked on the technical fix, the other kept stakeholders informed and coordinated with dependent teams.

E. Beyond Recovery: Building Business Continuity

A media company I worked with introduced me to an interesting metric they called “Time to Last Known Good State” (TLGS). Unlike traditional recovery time objectives, TLGS measured how quickly they could return to a fully functioning state from any type of failure. This shifted their thinking from reactive disaster recovery to proactive business continuity.

Their approach was born from a painful experience where a successful recovery still resulted in lost business. They had restored their systems quickly after a pipeline failure, but in the process, they lost several hours of customer data. Technically, the recovery was a success - they were back online within their target window. But from a business perspective, it was a failure.

This led them to develop what they called “state-aware recovery.” Every critical system maintained a continuous log of not just what state it was in, but what state it should be in. During recovery, they wouldn’t just restore systems - they would reconcile states across their entire platform. This meant they could recover not just their technical systems, but their business operations as well.

One particularly elegant aspect of their solution was their approach to customer communication during incidents. They created what they called “status stories” - continuously updated narratives of what was happening, what was being done about it, and what customers could expect. These weren’t just status updates; they were carefully crafted communications that helped maintain customer confidence even during major incidents.

The lesson that ties all of this together came from a CTO I worked with who said, “The true measure of a delivery system isn’t how often it succeeds - it’s how gracefully it fails and how quickly it recovers." In Continuous Delivery, building for failure is as important as building for success. Your pipeline isn't just a tool for delivering software; it's a critical business system that needs to be as resilient as any other part of your production infrastructure.

This perspective fundamentally changed how we approached pipeline design. We stopped trying to build perfect systems and instead focused on building recoverable ones. We replaced complex automated failover mechanisms with simple, well-documented manual procedures. We invested in training and practice rather than more automation. Most importantly, we recognized that our delivery pipeline was now as critical to our business as our production systems - and we started treating it that way.

Blueprint Summary

Continuous Delivery creates robust technical foundations that enable teams to ship high-quality software rapidly and reliably. Based on extensive experience implementing CD across organizations, here are the key elements for success:

1. **Pipeline Architecture: Your Delivery Foundation**
    - Automated builds and systematic testing
    - Reliable, repeatable deployment processes
    - Built-in redundancy and recovery mechanisms
    - Failure-resistant design principles
    - Clear paths for code to production
2. **Testing Framework: Your Quality Guardian**
    - Layered testing strategy from unit to end-to-end

- Quick developer feedback cycles
- Comprehensive journey validation
- Trust-building through verification
- Balance between coverage and speed

3. Infrastructure Management: Your Stable Base
    - Infrastructure as code practices
    - Automated environment creation
    - Self-healing system capabilities
    - Consistent delivery environments
    - Scalable resource management
4. Release Management: Your Deployment Control
    - Feature flags for controlled rollouts
    - Canary releases for risk reduction
    - Blue-green deployment strategies
    - Quick rollback capabilities
    - Safe production change processes
5. Monitoring & Feedback: Your Early Warning System
    - Real-time system visibility
    - Predictive problem detection
    - Performance tracking
    - User impact monitoring
    - Continuous improvement loops

6. **Disaster Recovery: Your Business Continuity Shield**
    - Clear recovery procedures
    - Regular practice drills
    - Business operation protection
    - Fast incident response
    - System resilience planning

Success in Continuous Delivery requires balancing technical excellence with operational resilience. Your pipeline isn't just a deployment tool—it's a critical business system that deserves the same care and planning as your production environment. When implemented effectively, CD creates a competitive advantage by enabling consistent, reliable value delivery to customers, even in challenging circumstances.

Conclusion

The journey to Continuous Delivery excellence is both technical and human. While robust automation and well-designed systems form the foundation, success ultimately depends on how well teams respond to challenges and recover from setbacks. The most successful organizations understand that Continuous Delivery isn't just about deploying code faster – it's about building resilient systems and processes that can weather any storm.

Building an effective Continuous Delivery pipeline requires careful attention to both technical excellence and operational resilience. The foundation you build must not only support your current needs but also provide clear paths to recovery when issues arise. Your delivery pipeline isn't just an automation tool – it's a critical business system that deserves the same level of care and planning as your production environment.

As we move into Chapter 3: AGILITY, we'll explore how team organization and work management practices complement these technical capabilities. We'll see how agile methodologies help teams respond to change effectively, whether that change comes from new feature requests or unexpected system failures. The combination of robust technical practices and adaptable team structures creates an environment where innovation can flourish while maintaining operational stability.

This holistic approach to Continuous Delivery – embracing both technical excellence and operational resilience – sets the stage for sustainable growth. When your pipeline is not only fast and reliable but also resilient and recoverable, you create a true competitive advantage that enables your startup to deliver value to customers consistently, even in the face of challenges.

Put These Ideas Into Action

Get your free unicorn Blueprint Field Guide with templates & worksheets

Scan the QR code or visit the URL below to access your resources
https://scaleupmethodology.com/the-unicorn-blueprint-fieldguide/

Chapter No. 3

AGILITY: Flex, Adapt, and Dominate

I. The Agility Imperative

As I stood at the back of yet another startup pitch event in Riyadh, a familiar pattern emerged - one I had seen countless times since arriving in Saudi Arabia. Startup after startup took the stage, each proudly introducing their team. "Here's our CTO, our CFO, and of course, our Project Manager," they would say. But time and time again, I found myself asking the same question: Where was the Chief Product Officer?

This observation wasn't limited to startup pitches. At technology conferences across the Kingdom, I've been struck by the overwhelming pride in PMP (Project Management Professional) certifications. Attendees would eagerly display their PMP credentials, viewing them as a badge of honor and a key to success in the tech world.

Don't get me wrong - project management skills are valuable.

But as I listened to these startups outline their plans with detailed Gantt charts and milestone-heavy roadmaps, I couldn't help but think of a quote often attributed to Mike Tyson: "Everyone has a plan until they get punched in the mouth."

Let's visualize the key differences between traditional and agile approaches to understand why agility is crucial in today's fast-paced startup environment:

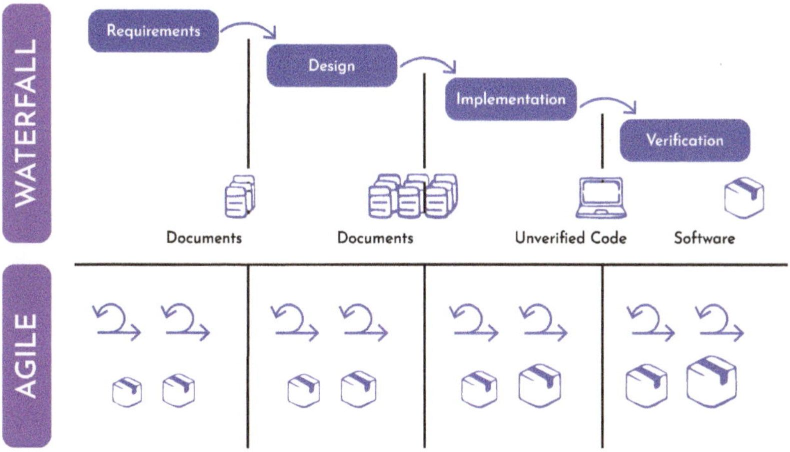

As we can see from this comparison, traditional approaches emphasize upfront planning and rigid execution, while agile methodologies enable continuous adaptation and learning. The rigid hierarchies and detailed Gantt charts of traditional project management contrast sharply with the iterative cycles and feedback loops of agile development. This fundamental difference in approach determines how effectively an organization can respond to change.

In the world of digital product development and scaling startups, that punch often comes in the form of rapidly changing market conditions, evolving customer needs, or disruptive new technologies. And when that punch lands, no amount of traditional project management can save you if you lack the agility to adapt.

This clash of mindsets isn't unique to Saudi Arabia. I've seen it in the automotive strongholds of Germany, in the financial centers of London, and even in traditional banking institutions of Portugal. The common thread? A misunderstanding of what agility really means, and why it's crucial for success in the digital age.

Agility isn't about being fast for the sake of speed. It's not about cutting corners or skipping planning. True agility is about creating an organization that can sense and respond to change quickly. It's about building a culture of continuous learning and adaptation. And for scaling startups, it's the difference between explosive growth and stagnation.

I remember one particular conference where I was invited to speak about agile methodologies. After my talk, a young entrepreneur approached me, his PMP certificate prominently displayed on his lanyard. "But how can we plan for agility?" he asked, genuinely puzzled. "How can we create a Gantt chart for being flexible?"

His question encapsulated the fundamental misunderstanding that I've encountered so often. The methods that work for building bridges or managing construction projects can be disastrous when applied to the fluid, fast-paced world of digital products and scaling startups.

The roots of this misunderstanding often lie in the different nature of the problems being solved. Traditional project management excels in environments where the problem is well-defined, the solution is known, and the path to that solution can be clearly mapped out. This works well for construction projects, manufacturing processes, or other endeavors where the end result is clearly specified from the start.

But in the world of startups and digital products, we're often dealing with what are known as "wicked problems" - complex issues that are difficult or impossible to solve because of incomplete, contradictory, and changing requirements that are often difficult to recognize. The solution to a wicked problem is often not true or false, but better or worse. And the nature of the problem isn't fully understood until after the formulation of a solution.

This is why traditional, plan-driven approaches often fall short in the startup world. They assume a level of predictability and stability that simply doesn't exist when you're trying to create something new and innovative in a rapidly changing market.

Agile methodologies, on the other hand, are designed specifically to deal with uncertainty and change. They acknowledge that we don't have all the answers up front, and that our understanding of both the problem and the solution will evolve over time. They emphasize rapid iteration, continuous feedback, and the ability to change direction quickly based on new information.

This is not to say that planning is not important in agile environments. On the contrary, Agile involves comprehensive planning at multiple levels - from the high-level Product Vision that sets overall direction, down through the Product Roadmap and Release plans, to detailed Sprint planning for the next two weeks, and finally to Daily planning in stand-ups. This hierarchical approach to planning allows teams to maintain strategic alignment while staying flexible and adaptive. Instead of creating rigid long-term plans, they maintain a clear vision for the future while focusing on detailed planning for shorter increments, enabling them to adjust course as they learn more about their market, customers, and product.

In this chapter, we're going to dive deep into the world of agility. We'll explore what it really means to be agile, why it's critical for scaling startups, and how to foster agility in your organization. We'll look at practical methodologies, tools, and mindset shifts required to embrace agility fully. And we'll do it all through the lens of real-world experiences and hard-won lessons.

So, whether you're a founder struggling to maintain your startup's early dynamism as you scale, or an executive trying to inject agility into a more traditional organization, this chapter is for you. Are you ready to flex, adapt, and dominate your market? Let's dive in and unlock the power of agility.

Now that we understand why agility is crucial in today's rapidly evolving startup landscape, let's clarify exactly what we mean by agility in the context of scaling companies. As with many powerful concepts, agility is often misunderstood - and this misunderstanding can lead to costly mistakes as you scale.

II. Defining Agility in the Context of Scaling Startups

Before we dive into the how of agility, let's take a moment to clarify what we mean by this often-misunderstood term. In my travels, I've found that "agility" is often used interchangeably with "speed" or "chaos." Both of these interpretations miss the mark and can lead to disastrous consequences for scaling startups.

Agility, in the context of scaling startups, is the ability to respond quickly and effectively to changes in the market, customer needs, and internal conditions. It's about creating an organization that can learn and adapt rapidly, without losing sight of its core mission and values.

Key characteristics of agility include:

1. **Iterative approach:** Breaking work into small, manageable chunks and continuously refining based on feedback.
2. **Customer-centricity:** Keeping the focus on delivering value to customers, rather than following rigid plans.
3. **Embracing change:** Seeing change as an opportunity rather than a threat.
4. **Empowered teams:** Giving teams the authority and resources to make decisions and act quickly.
5. **Continuous learning:** Fostering a culture of experimentation and learning from both successes and failures.

These five characteristics form an interconnected system that creates true organizational agility. Let's examine how they work together:

THE FIVE PILLARS OF AGILITY

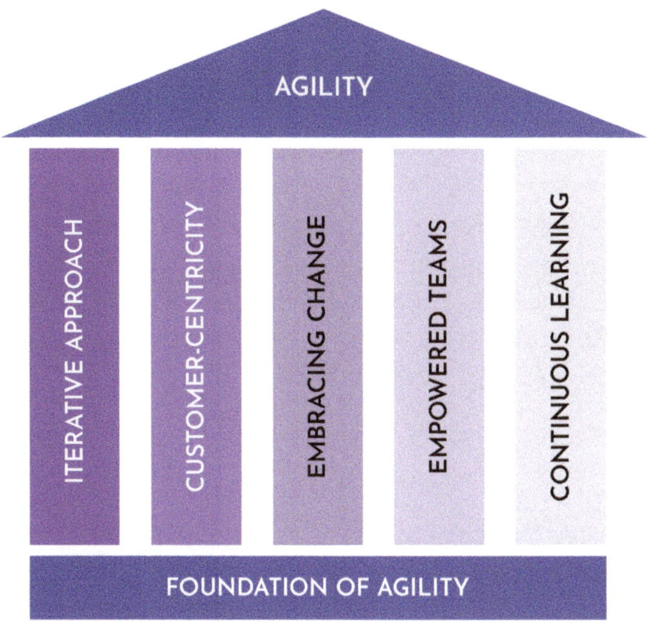

At the center lies True Agility, supported and enabled by these five key characteristics. Notice how each element connects to and reinforces the others - iterative approaches enable customer-centricity through frequent feedback, while empowered teams drive continuous learning, and embracing change becomes possible through this interconnected system. This holistic view helps us understand why implementing just one or two elements isn't enough - true agility requires all five working in harmony.

Let me illustrate this with a story from my consulting days. I once worked with a startup that prided itself on its "agility." They would pivot their entire business model every few weeks based on the latest market trends. They moved fast, but they were directionless. Their employees were exhausted, their customers were confused, and their investors were losing patience.

This wasn't agility - it was chaos.

We implemented true agile practices, starting with defining a clear vision and strategy. We broke down their work into two-week sprints, each with a specific goal tied to their overall mission. We implemented regular customer feedback sessions and retrospectives to learn and adjust course as needed.

The result? Within three months, they had a stable product direction, happier employees, and were actually making progress towards their goals. They were moving more deliberately, but they were moving in the right direction. That's the power of true agility.

But what does this look like in practice? Let's break it down further:

1. **Iterative Approach:** Instead of trying to build the perfect product in one go, agile teams work in short cycles (often called sprints) of 1-4 weeks. At the end of each cycle,

they have a working piece of software that delivers some value, even if it's not the full vision. This allows them to get feedback early and often, and to course-correct if needed.

For example, instead of spending six months building a full-featured app, they might release a basic version after two weeks, add the next most important feature in the following two weeks, and so on. This way, if they discover after a month that users aren't interested in a particular feature they had planned, they haven't wasted months building something nobody wants.

2. **Customer-centricity:** Agile teams put the customer at the center of everything they do. They're not just building features because they're on a roadmap, but because they solve real customer problems. This often involves regular customer interviews, usability testing, and analyzing usage data to understand what customers really need and value.

I once worked with a team that was building a productivity app. They had a long list of features they thought were important, but when we started doing regular user testing, we discovered that most users only cared about one or two core features. By focusing on perfecting those features instead of building a dozen mediocre ones, they were able to create a product that users loved and recommended to others.

3. **Embracing Change:** In traditional project management, change is often seen as a risk to be mitigated. In agile, change is seen as an opportunity to create something better. This doesn't mean blindly accepting every change request, but rather being open to new information and willing to adjust plans when it makes sense.

For instance, I worked with a startup that was building a

B2B software product. Halfway through development, they received feedback from a potential major client that if the product had one additional feature, they would sign a large contract. In a traditional approach, adding this feature might have been seen as scope creep and rejected. But because they were working in an agile way, they were able to reprioritize their backlog, add this high-value feature, and secure a game-changing client.

4. **Empowered Teams:** Agile teams are typically cross-functional, meaning they have all the skills needed to take an idea from concept to production. They're also empowered to make decisions about how to best achieve their goals, rather than having to get approval for every small decision.

In one startup I advised, we reorganized their structure from functional departments (separate teams for design, development, QA, etc.) to cross-functional product teams. Each team was responsible for a specific part of the product and had the authority to make decisions about it. This not only sped up their development process but also increased employee satisfaction as people felt more ownership over their work.

5. **Continuous Learning:** Agile teams build learning into their process. They don't just deliver work; they regularly step back to reflect on how they can improve. This is often done through practices like sprint retrospectives, where the team discusses what went well, what didn't, and what they can do better next time.

I remember working with a team that initially resisted the idea of retrospectives, seeing them as a waste of time. But after a few sessions where they identified and fixed some major bottlenecks in their process, they became enthusiastic supporters. Over time, this habit of continuous improvement led to significant gains in both productivity and quality.

It's important to note that agility isn't just about adopting a set of practices or following a specific methodology. It's a mindset - a way of approaching work that emphasizes flexibility, collaboration, and continuous improvement. The specific practices a team uses might vary, but if they embody these principles, they're on the path to true agility.

Understanding what agility means is just the first step. The real challenge lies in making the fundamental mindset shift required to embrace agility fully. This shift begins with challenging one of the most deeply ingrained assumptions in business: the idea that we need a perfect, detailed vision before we can start executing.v

III. Perfect vs. Blurred Vision

For founders scaling their startups, one of the most crucial mindset shifts is moving away from the traditional Waterfall practice that many business visions are founded on in the pre-digital era. Under the traditional, industrial age model, a founder begins the process of development with a perfect vision of the desired outcomes, versus Agile which is intentionally blurred from the outset but leaves itself the space and time to develop that vision.

I was particularly struck by Jeff Patton's "Don't know what I want, but I know how to get it" observation that iterating and incrementing are separate ideas. Using Waterfall, Patton explains that an artist, such as Da Vinci, would begin a process with a complete picture of the Mona Lisa in mind. He explains that had he used the Waterfall approach, Da Vinci would have painted the perfect portrait of the Mona Lisa that we all recognize today that replicated his initial vision.

However, in reality, Da Vinci would have constructed that portrait iteratively, building it segment by segment and redrawing as each new element was added, until finally, the portrait appeared as the masterpiece it is.

Let's visualize this iterative process to understand how it differs from the traditional waterfall approach:

Incrementing Towards a Fully Formed Idea - Waterfall

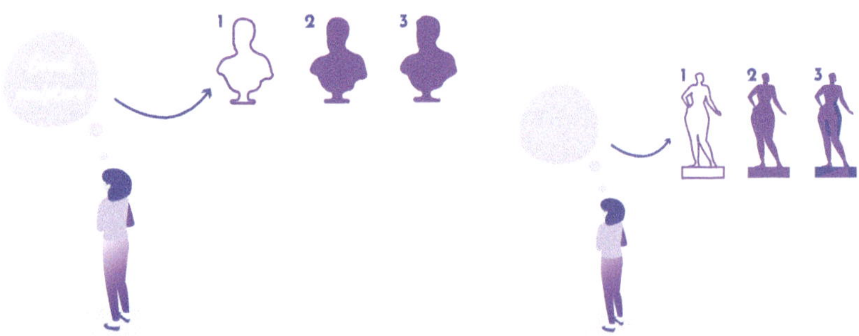

Iterating Ideas - Agile

Following the sequence from left to right, we can see how each iteration builds upon and refines the previous one. The arrows between panels represent feedback loops, where learning from each stage informs improvements in the next. This iterative approach allows for continuous refinement and adaptation, unlike the rigid waterfall method that attempts to plan everything perfectly from the start.

Imagine if today's scaling startups applied Waterfall to creating their products – the founders and their teams would need to start from a point of complete certainty and perfect vision. It would be untested and un-validated by the time it was released into the market or operations of a business. All that detailed planning from the outset might be worth nothing if that product is then deemed irrelevant and unworkable for its intended user base.

Instead, the Agile way begins with an intent to achieve a goal, but it's not the perfect finished version – it's more blurred. Using an Agile, iterative and incremental development process helps achieve that goal by knowing what's desired as an outcome within a landscape that is constantly shifting and evolving.

Let me illustrate this through another powerful analogy that resonates with founders. Consider how the world moved on from taking photographs on film, taking the roll to the printers, waiting for it to be developed before seeing the results printed on paper. How many times has that final, developed image been spoiled by a thumb in shot, or the photo is out of focus, or badly framed? By the time the finished photo is ready, it's too late, the moment has passed, and what was hoped to be a perfect memory is subsequently tossed aside and discarded.

Today, photography is instant, thanks to digital technology. The goal remains the same – to capture an image via a lens but the process is a thousand times faster, and allows the photographer to change and adapt in real time until they are satisfied they have captured the image to their liking. This perfectly encapsulates the difference between traditional and agile approaches to startup scaling.

In scaling startups, the Waterfall approach relies on setting that perfect image of the product/service from the very beginning, and then investing inordinate amounts of time, effort and resources in achieving that. However, what happens when it's released into the market after such a lengthy development process but it's not up to par, or is out-bested by a similar competitive product? It's tossed aside and discarded and the investment is wasted. Not all the time, of course, but for startups, Waterfall naturally carries risk, which can be catastrophic when runway is limited.

Times have indeed changed and founders are no longer bound by the perfect Waterfall visions that suited the industrial age. The digital-age-savvy startup leaders that understand the power of agility thrive in a landscape filled with opportunities that they're eager and willing to exploit to their maximum potential. Agility is not simply a fancy word steeped in business philosophy; it's that mindset I referred to which sets successful scaleups apart.

Of course, quite possibly you as a founder are already familiar with the term "Agile" in the business sense, but haven't yet given it much consideration beyond being a buzzword that has little, or no relevance to your scaling practice. Or, if you have adopted Agile, you still may not have reaped its reward, or fully understood its full potential, especially if it was introduced as a tick box exercise to enhance 'training'. In that respect, it's often viewed as a badge of excellence. However, if it's not fully embedded as an ongoing process that is continually reviewed, refreshed and redrawn at regular intervals, it never has the opportunity to shine right across the whole startup.

This is the main reason why I want founders and startup leaders to understand that agility – and Agile – is a mindset that begins with them. It's not simply a process that should be delegated to a consultant expert for the IT department. Agility is a state of mind and it must be founder-led. Agile then works best when it's applied cross-functionally, not just at team level. Left within a departmental silo (as often is the case) eventually it will suffocate. However, when a startup leader understands the benefits that agility delivers, Agile has the potential to accelerate value delivery. Agility also maximises opportunities for the business to react and respond quickly, such as when Facebook (no stranger to agility), increased its capacity to provide video calling features during the Covid-19 pandemic to compete with Zoom's conferencing product. Facebook consequently adapted and added several new video-calling features to its subsidiary brands of WhatsApp and Messenger as well as to its main app, following increased demand for social video calling, temporarily sending the Zoom share price tumbling.

The reality is that for scaling startups, if your business still uses Waterfall as a process, it's completely surrounded by the Agile world around it and it's hemmed in. That's why I urge all startup leaders to rethink it as a strategy because Waterfall is no longer relevant in the current environment, given that competitors are reading and responding to market conditions so quickly. Given that every scaling startup is its own complex world, it's impossible in today's environment to run it along the industrial era principles of Waterfall.

Therefore, even if you've built initial traction for your startup using traditional approaches, that success will, in all probability, be unsustainable as you try to scale, especially in today's rapidly changing market conditions. Startup leaders, if they wish to avoid that, must accept a paradigm shift in thinking if they wish to remain relevant and no longer wish to struggle to survive. Agile is that mindset and not a quick fix process to dig a business from out of a hole.

While the benefits of an agile mindset might seem theoretical, the costs of remaining rigid are very real. To understand just how devastating a lack of agility can be, even for established companies, let's look at a concrete example from my experience at Nokia - a cautionary tale that holds valuable lessons for scaling startups.

IV. The Cost of Rigidity

To truly understand the importance of agility, sometimes it's helpful to look at what happens when it's absent. Let me share a story from my time at Nokia, a company that was once at the forefront of mobile technology but struggled to adapt to the smartphone era.

In 2009, I changed departments within Nokia and was hired to completely overhaul the localization process for Nokia Maps. At that time, the entire localization process was done using a waterfall approach. This meant that all development was completed before localization even began. We're talking about translating Nokia Maps into more than 90 languages - a process that typically took 3-4 months.

Imagine the scenario: after months of development, we would then spend 3-4 months translating everything, building all the packages, and then testing all the languages. Inevitably, bugs would be found, requiring fixes, rebuilds, and retesting. The entire process could stretch to 4-5 months.

Let's compare the traditional waterfall approach with the agile process we implemented:

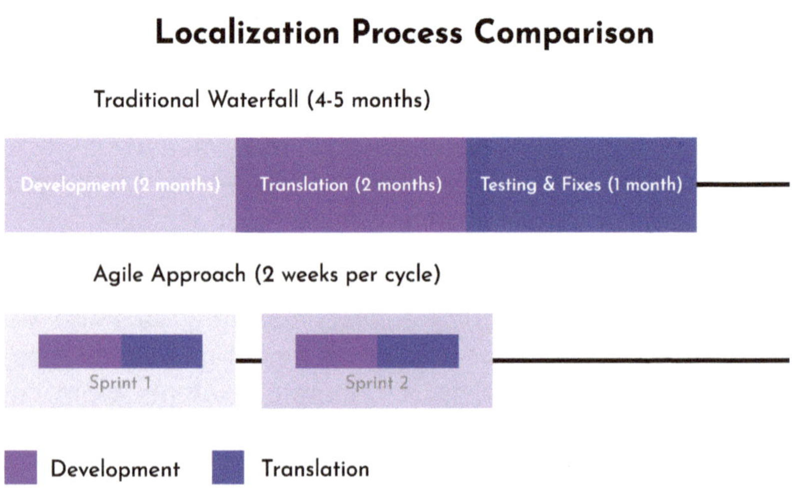

The contrast between these approaches is stark. In the waterfall timeline, we see long periods of sequential work with delays and bottlenecks. The agile timeline shows concurrent development and localization, with shorter cycles and faster feedback loops. The red sections in the waterfall timeline highlight the periods of waiting and rework that were eliminated in the agile approach.

For a company like Nokia, waiting 4-5 months was problematic but manageable. But for a startup? This kind of delay could be catastrophic. It's a perfect example of how old waterfall processes can destroy your company's agility and, by extension, its ability to compete in a fast-moving market.

Let's break down the problems with this approach:

1. **Delayed Feedback:** By waiting until the end of development to start localization, we were delaying valuable feedback. What if certain features didn't translate well into other languages or cultures? We wouldn't know until months after the feature was developed.

2. **Inflexibility:** If market conditions changed or new competitors emerged during the 4-5 month localization process, we couldn't easily adapt. The product was essentially frozen during this time.

3. **Increased Risk:** By doing all the localization at once, we were increasing the risk of the project. If something went wrong, it could affect all 90+ languages.

4. **Delayed Time-to-Market:** In the fast-moving world of technology, a 4-5 month delay can be the difference between being a market leader and an also-ran.

5. **Resource Inefficiency:** The waterfall approach led to boom-and-bust cycles in resource utilization. The

localization team would be overwhelmed for a few months, then potentially underutilized until the next big push.

My job was to integrate the translation process into the development sprints. Instead of waiting until the end, we would get a list of features to be implemented at the beginning of each sprint, along with all the strings that needed to be localized. These strings would be sent to the translation vendor and returned within the sprint.

By the end of the sprint, we had features that were completely localized. They weren't fully tested - that would happen in the following sprint - but the bulk of the work was done. We reduced the waiting time from 4 months to a couple of weeks after development. And the quality improvements were substantial. When you wait to collect all the strings at the end of the process, many things change, and many strings get missed, leading to a costly back-and-forth.

The benefits of this new approach were numerous:

1. **Faster Time-to-Market:** We could now release localized versions of Nokia Maps much more quickly, keeping pace with the rapid changes in the mobile market.

2. **Improved Quality:** By integrating localization into the development process, we caught and fixed issues much earlier, leading to a higher quality end product.

3. **Greater Flexibility:** If market conditions changed or new requirements emerged, we could adapt much more quickly. We weren't locked into a months-long localization process.

4. **Better Resource Utilization:** The localization work was now spread out more evenly, leading to more consistent and efficient use of resources.

5. **Reduced Risk:** By localizing in smaller batches, we reduced the risk of large-scale failures. If issues arose, they were contained to a smaller set of features and languages.
6. **Improved Collaboration:** The new process fostered better collaboration between developers and localizers, leading to a product that was designed from the ground up to work well in multiple languages and cultures.

This experience was so impactful that I even wrote my master's thesis on the importance of agility in localization processes. It demonstrated to me the power of agile principles, not just in software development, but in adjacent processes as well.

The lesson here is clear: agility isn't just about moving fast. It's about integrating processes that traditionally happen in sequence, getting feedback early and often, and being able to adapt quickly to changes. For startups, this kind of agility can be the difference between success and failure.

But it's not just about the processes - it's about the mindset. The agile approach we implemented at Nokia required a significant shift in how people thought about their work. Developers had to consider localization from the start, rather than as an afterthought. Localizers had to be ready to work in smaller, more frequent batches rather than in one big push.

This mindset shift is often the hardest part of becoming agile. It requires people to let go of the illusion of certainty that traditional approaches provide. Instead of having a detailed plan for the next several months, teams need to become comfortable with uncertainty and adapt as they go.

For startups, this agile mindset is crucial. The startup world is inherently uncertain. You're often creating something new, entering untested markets, or disrupting established industries. You don't have the luxury of spending months on detailed plans that may become obsolete as soon as they're finished.

Instead, you need to be able to move quickly, learn from your mistakes, and adapt your approach based on real-world feedback. This is where agility shines. It gives you the tools and mindset to navigate uncertainty, to fail fast and learn quickly, and to continuously improve your product and your processes.

In the next section, we'll explore how this agile approach can have a direct impact on a startup's bottom line. We'll look at a financial case study that demonstrates why agility isn't just a nice-to-have for startups - it's a financial imperative.

The Nokia story illustrates the organizational costs of rigidity, but what about the bottom line? For scaling startups, understanding the financial implications of agility versus rigidity is crucial. Let's examine how an agile approach can dramatically impact your startup's financial health and value delivery.

V. The Financial Impact and Value Delivery of Agility

Now, let's talk about money and value delivery - two sides of the same coin that are critical for scaling startups. After all, for startups, cash is king, and your ability to deliver value quickly can mean the difference between success and failure. Let me walk you through one of the most powerful examples I use in my classes to demonstrate why agility isn't just a nice-to-have - it's a financial imperative for any scaling business.

The Financial Case for Agility

Imagine you have a team of 5 people, each earning €5,000 a month. You're taking 12 months to develop your product. As soon as the product is ready after 12 months, you start generating revenue of €100,000 a month. Let's calculate the cash flow of the company.

In the traditional waterfall model:

- **Development costs:** 5 people * €5,000 * 12 months = €300,000
- **Revenue starts at month 13:** €100,000 per month
- **Break-even point:** Month 15

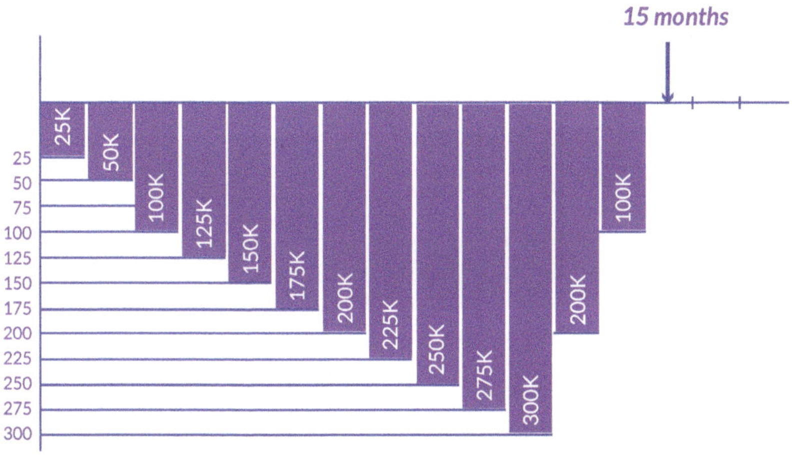

Now, let's look at the same scenario using agile methodologies, releasing increments every quarter:

- **Quarter 1:** €25,000 revenue per month
- **Quarter 2:** €50,000 revenue per month
- **Quarter 3:** €75,000 revenue per month
- **Quarter 4:** €100,000 revenue per month

In this scenario, you reach break-even by the 8th month. That's a seven-month difference! This example illustrates a crucial point: agility doesn't necessarily make things faster. The product still takes 12 months to fully develop. But by releasing increments and generating revenue earlier, you dramatically improve your cash flow position.

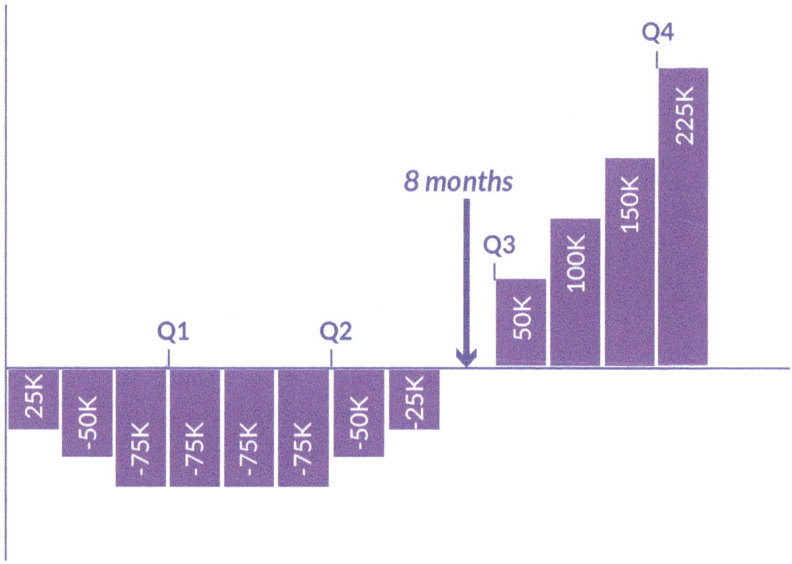

The Value Delivery Advantage

From a value delivery perspective, Agile creates a continuous stream that enables money to flow faster - a critical consideration for scaling startups where runway is always a concern. For example, with software development in a scaling startup, it's possible to incrementally release 5% of the intended final product within as little as three months since its start-up development into the marketplace, yet it's still 100% usable.

Of course, there may not be the same full functionality that it will eventually have twelve months down the line, but by releasing it into the market sooner at a lower introductory price, it's possible to begin generating revenue and customer feedback.

This can have a huge impact on improved cash flow, compared to Waterfall and its requirement for up to one year of full salaries. Agile only depends on sponsoring two or three months of salaries up front, after which the business can incrementally charge more and more for its delivery.

Let's break down why this matters so much for scaling startups:

1. Runway Extension

    - For most startups, runway (the amount of time until you run out of money) is a constant concern
    - By generating revenue earlier, you're effectively extending your runway
    - This can be the difference between having to raise another round of funding (and dilute your equity) or reaching profitability on your current funding
    - Early revenue can help fund ongoing development, reducing reliance on external funding

2. Reduced Risk

    - In the waterfall model, you're taking on 12 months of risk before you see any return
    - Market conditions could change dramatically during that time
    - Competitors might beat you to market
    - In the agile model, you're reducing risk exposure by getting to market faster
    - You can validate assumptions with real customer feedback before committing significant resources

3. **Faster Learning**
   - Getting a version of your product to market in three months instead of 12 accelerates your learning cycle
   - Start gathering real user data and feedback much earlier
   - Make informed decisions about future development based on actual usage
   - Avoid building features that users don't want or need
4. **Investor Confidence**
   - For startups seeking additional funding, showing early traction is crucial
   - Being able to demonstrate revenue and user growth after just a few months is powerful
   - Much more compelling than asking investors to wait a full year for results
   - Shows ability to execute and adapt based on market feedback
5. **Competitive Advantage**
   - In many markets, especially in tech, being first can provide a significant advantage
   - Even if your initial product isn't fully featured, being first to market helps establish brand recognition
   - Start building a user base before competitors arrive
   - Create switching costs that make it harder for competitors to steal your customers

The Leadership Imperative

I am happy to repeat myself when I say the journey towards agility begins with you, the founder, so that you act as the example that everyone involved in the business can then follow. If you're not the one executing your own ideas that will send out a very clear message that the strategy lacks real substance and that agility is little more than a slogan.

The most successful scaleups that I've seen are those that have very inspiring founders that totally commit to what they tell their colleagues as well as re-organizing completely different, away from old practices associated with the industrial era. For scaling companies, this requires a more holistic approach which breaks down inter-departmental rivalries and instead fosters collaboration between them.

The outcome is that this shift in mindset leads to creating an organisation that focuses on products and services where the customer is placed at the center of everything. Your leadership in this respect is what will connect your vision with overall strategy, enabling your business to incrementally adapt, grow, become more competitive and cutting-edge in its mission to serve your customers.

Implementation in Practice

Let me share a real example from my consulting work. I recently worked with a SaaS startup that was building a complex enterprise product. Their initial plan was to spend 18 months building the "perfect" product before release. After analyzing their burn rate and market conditions, we shifted to an agile approach:

1. **Month 1-3:**
    - Released basic version with core functionality

- Started generating €20,000 monthly revenue
- Gathered crucial user feedback

2. **Month 4-6:**
    - Added features based on user needs
    - Revenue increased to €45,000 monthly
    - Started attracting larger clients
3. **Month 7-9:**
    - Implemented enterprise features
    - Revenue grew to €80,000 monthly
    - Secured Series A funding on better terms

The result? They reached profitability three months earlier than projected, raised funding at a higher valuation due to proven traction, and built exactly what their customers needed rather than what they initially assumed would be valuable.

This example demonstrates how agile value delivery impacts every aspect of a scaling startup:

- Financial health through earlier revenue
- Product-market fit through continuous feedback
- Fundraising success through demonstrated traction
- Team morale through visible progress
- Market position through faster iteration

The key to success is understanding that agile value delivery isn't just about development methodology - it's a comprehensive approach to building and scaling your business. It's about creating tight feedback loops between your team, your customers, and your market, then using those insights to make better decisions faster.

While the financial benefits of agility are compelling, many founders worry about the risks of changing their approach, especially during the critical scaling phase. However, as we'll see, maintaining rigid processes actually increases risk in today's fast-moving markets. Let's explore how to reduce risk through proper planning cadence and adaptive frameworks.

VI. Risk Reduction and Planning Cadence in Scaling

As a founder scaling your startup, you might feel understandably anxious about making major changes to your development and delivery processes. In adopting a huge paradigm shift in both your thinking and practice during the scaling phase, you may be concerned that any such change carries a risk. In one sense, that's true - people generally don't like change, it can make them feel uncertain or anxious. However, in today's rapidly evolving market, the greater risk lies in making no change at all.

The Real Risk Equation

Let me be clear: the most dangerous risk for scaling startups isn't in moving too fast - it's in moving too slowly or too rigidly. Consider these scenarios:

Traditional Approach (Higher Risk):

- 12 months of development before market feedback
- Full salary burn with no revenue

- One big bet on initial assumptions
- Market could change completely before launch
- Competitors could beat you to market

Agile Approach (Managed Risk):

- Feedback within 2-3 months
- Early revenue to offset costs
- Multiple small bets based on real data
- Continuous market alignment
- Ability to outmaneuver competitors

The key insight here is that risk reduction in scaling startups comes not from trying to plan everything perfectly upfront, but from creating systems that allow you to adapt quickly based on real-world feedback.

Implementing Risk-Reduction Strategies

Here are the practical steps I've seen work for scaling startups:

1. **Break Down Big Bets**
    - Split large initiatives into smaller experiments
    - Test critical assumptions early
    - Limit resource commitment until validation
    - Create clear success criteria for each experiment
2. **Build Feedback Loops**
    - Engage with customers continuously, not just at launch

- Monitor usage metrics in real-time
- Create channels for immediate user feedback
- Regularly assess market conditions and competitor moves

3. **Maintain Strategic Flexibility**
    - Keep options open as long as possible
    - Make decisions at the last responsible moment
    - Build in the ability to pivot based on new information
    - Reserve resources for opportunistic moves

The Power of Planning Cadence

One of the most effective tools for managing risk while maintaining momentum is implementing a proper planning cadence. Rather than creating one big plan upfront, scaling startups need a rhythmic cycle of planning and adjustment.

Here's how to implement an effective planning cadence:

1. **Quarterly Strategic Planning**
    - Review and adjust overall direction
    - Set clear objectives for the next quarter
    - Allocate resources based on latest learnings
    - Identify major risks and opportunities
2. **Monthly Alignment**
    - Check progress against quarterly objectives
    - Make necessary course corrections

- Update priorities based on new information
- Ensure teams remain coordinated

3. **Weekly Execution**
    - Review immediate priorities
    - Address emerging issues
    - Share learnings across teams
    - Plan next week's key activities
4. **Daily Coordination**
    - Quick team synchronization
    - Identify and remove blockers
    - Share critical updates
    - Maintain momentum

This nested planning approach allows you to maintain strategic direction while staying responsive to change. It's particularly crucial for scaling startups, where market conditions and customer expectations can shift rapidly.

Managing Customer Expectations

Remember that your "customer" may be internal - such as teams or departments who will use what you're building - or external end users. Both require careful attention to need and expectation:

Internal Customers:

- Regular check-ins with stakeholders
- Clear communication about progress and changes

- Quick response to urgent needs
- Balanced prioritization across departments

External Customers:

- Transparent communication about roadmap
- Early access programs for key customers
- Regular feedback sessions
- Clear expectation setting about features and timing

Planning Cadence in Practice

Before we dive into a practical example, let's visualize how different planning horizons work together in an agile organization:

Planning Cadence Hierarchy

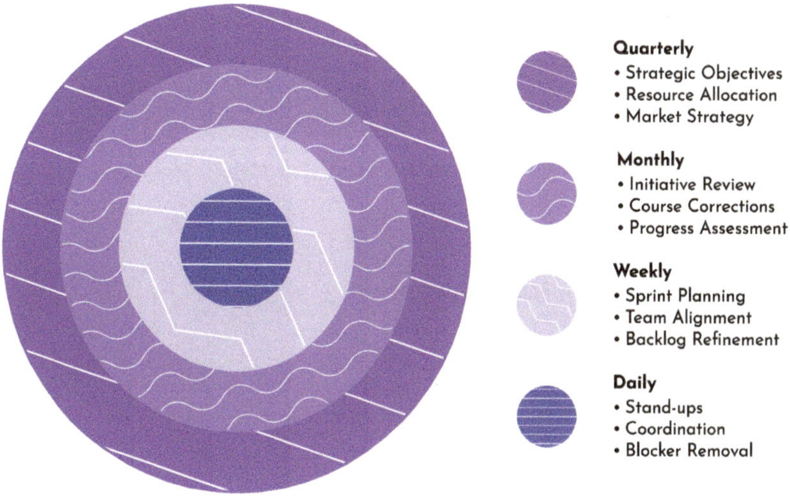

This diagram shows how planning operates at different time scales, from daily coordination at the center to quarterly strategic planning at the outer ring. Each layer builds upon and supports the others, creating a coherent planning system that maintains both strategic direction and tactical flexibility. The lighter colors in the outer rings represent increasing levels of abstraction and flexibility in planning horizons.

Let me share a concrete example from a scaling fintech startup I worked with. They shifted from quarterly releases to this cadence:

Weekly:

- Monday: Team planning meetings
- Daily: 15-minute coordination standups
- Thursday: Customer feedback sessions
- Friday: Week review and next week prep

Monthly:

- First week: Monthly planning
- Mid-month: Progress review
- Last week: Preparation for next month
- Continuous: Stakeholder updates

The results were transformative:

- Release frequency increased 4x
- Customer satisfaction improved 40%
- Team burnout reduced significantly
- Market responsiveness dramatically improved

The Flexible Framework

For scaling startups, the key is creating what I call a "flexible framework" - a structure that provides enough guidance to keep everyone aligned while maintaining the flexibility to adapt quickly. **This means:**

1. **Clear but Adaptable Processes**
    - Documented but not rigid
    - Regular review and refinement
    - Focus on principles over procedures
    - Built-in mechanisms for change
2. **Balanced Metrics**
    - Leading and lagging indicators
    - Customer and business metrics
    - Short and long-term measures
    - Qualitative and quantitative data
3. **Empowered Decision-Making**
    - Clear decision rights
    - Distributed authority
    - Rapid escalation paths
    - Regular decision reviews

By implementing these practices, scaling startups can significantly reduce their risk while maintaining their ability to move quickly and decisively. The goal isn't to eliminate risk - that's impossible in the startup world. Instead, it's about creating systems that help you identify, understand,

and respond to risks effectively while keeping your team aligned and motivated.

Remember, the most successful scaling startups aren't the ones that avoid all risks - they're the ones that get better at taking the right risks in the right ways. Your planning cadence should support this goal, providing the structure needed to scale while maintaining the flexibility to adapt and evolve as circumstances change.

Having explored the mindset, implementation, and practical benefits of agility, let's synthesize these insights into a clear framework you can use to transform your scaling startup. The following blueprint captures the essential elements needed to build a truly agile organization."

Blueprint Summary

Agility enables startups to adapt and evolve while maintaining momentum, creating sustainable growth through rapid adaptation and value delivery. Here are the essential elements for success:

1. **Mindset Foundation:** Embracing Flexible Thinking
   - Shift from perfect planning to evolving vision
   - View uncertainty as opportunity, not threat
   - Focus on learning and adaptation
   - Build culture of continuous improvement
   - Lead agility from the top down
2. **Value Delivery Systems:** Creating Early Impact
   - Release incremental value frequently

- Generate early revenue streams
- Build tight customer feedback loops
- Balance short-term and long-term needs
- Iterate based on customer response

3. **Risk Management Framework:** Smart Risk Taking
    - Break large initiatives into small experiments
    - Validate assumptions early and often
    - Create clear adaptation points
    - Maintain strategic flexibility
    - Adjust course based on real data
4. **Planning and Execution:** Structured Flexibility
    - Implement nested planning cycles
    - Enable coordinated decision-making
    - Balance control with autonomy
    - Maintain strategic alignment
    - Adapt tactics to ground reality
5. **Leadership Practices:** Modeling Agile Behavior
    - Create psychological safety
    - Encourage experimentation
    - Foster cross-functional collaboration
    - Share knowledge freely
    - Balance standards with innovation

The journey to agility isn't about specific methodologies—it's about fundamentally changing how your organization thinks about and responds to change. Success comes from building an organization that can sense and respond to change quickly while maintaining strategic direction. This balance between stability and flexibility enables sustainable scaling.

Conclusion

The journey to agility is not about implementing specific methodologies or practices - it's about fundamentally changing how your organization thinks about and responds to change. For scaling startups, this transformation is not optional; it's a core requirement for survival and success in today's rapidly evolving markets.

Remember that the goal isn't to become "more agile" for its own sake. The goal is to build an organization capable of sensing and responding to change quickly while maintaining its strategic direction. This balance between stability and flexibility is what enables sustainable scaling.

As we move into Chapter 4: LUCRATIVE, we'll explore how this agile foundation directly impacts your financial success. While agility provides the framework for rapid adaptation and growth, it must translate into sustainable financial performance. The ability to move quickly and adapt to market changes is only valuable if it generates returns and creates lasting value.

The next chapter will dive deep into the financial practices needed to ensure your agile organization can scale profitably. We'll see how combining agile capabilities with strong financial management creates a powerful engine for sustainable growth. The marriage of agility and financial acumen enables your startup to not just move fast, but to move fast in ways that build lasting value.

Your agility journey begins with understanding that it's not about perfect execution of a predetermined plan - it's about building an organization that can learn and adapt faster than the competition while maintaining financial discipline. By implementing the principles and practices outlined in this chapter, you'll be well on your way to creating a truly agile organization capable of sustained, profitable scaling.

The transition from agility to financial management is natural - because ultimately, your ability to move quickly and adapt effectively must be grounded in sound financial practices. As we move forward to discuss the LUCRATIVE pillar, remember that agility provides the framework within which your startup can achieve both rapid growth and financial success.

Chapter No. 4

LUCRATIVE: Unlock Financial Mastery

I. The Financial Foundation of Scaling

As I stood in the conference room of a once-promising startup, the atmosphere was tense. The founders, who had been riding high on a wave of rapid growth and media attention, now faced a stark reality: they were three weeks away from running out of cash. Their product was gaining traction, their team was talented, but they had fallen into a common trap - rigid annual budgets allocated to departments rather than value delivery, making it impossible to adapt quickly to market changes.

This scene, which I've witnessed more times than I care to count, underscores a critical truth in the world of startups: no matter how innovative your product or how brilliant your team, without modern financial management that enables agility and focuses on value delivery, your startup i.s built on sand.

The LUCRATIVE pillar of the Scaleup Methodology is about transforming your startup from a cash-burning machine into a sustainable, profitable business capable of long-term growth and success. But it goes beyond traditional financial management - it's about implementing dynamic funding models that align with how modern startups actually create and deliver value.

Before we dive in, let's address some common misconceptions about startup finances:

1. "Traditional annual budgeting works for startups." This couldn't be further from the truth. Annual budgets allocated to departments create artificial constraints and prevent rapid adaptation to market opportunities.

2. "We'll figure out the finances once we've grown." This "grow now, profit later" mentality has led countless startups to an early grave. Financial management isn't something you can postpone - it needs to be baked into your business from day one.

3. "Financial management is just about keeping track of expenses." While expense management is important, true financial mastery involves dynamic funding models aligned with value streams, participatory budgeting practices, and the ability to quickly reallocate resources where they'll generate the most value.

4. "We don't need to worry about finances because we've raised a lot of money." Even well-funded startups can crash and burn if they don't manage their resources wisely and align funding with value creation.

Financial Management Paradigm Shift

Traditional Approach	Modern Approach
Annual Budgeting Fixed yearly budgets with limited flexibility	**Dynamic Funding** Flexible, quarterly adjustments
Department-Based Siloed resources and decision-making	**Value Stream-Based** Resources aligned with value creation
Fixed Allocations Rigid resource distribution	**Adaptive Allocation** Quick reallocation to opportunities
Cost Control Focus Emphasis on expense management	**Value Creation Focus** Emphasis on growth and innovation

Understanding this shift in mindset is crucial - it's not just about changing processes, but about fundamentally transforming how we think about and manage resources in scaling startups.

Let me share a story that illustrates the power of modern financial management. I recently worked with a startup that had built a promising SaaS platform. They had a solid product and had raised significant funding, but were struggling to scale efficiently. Their traditional department-based budgeting was creating silos and slowing their ability to respond to market opportunities.

We helped them transition to a value stream-based funding model, where resources were allocated to customer-centric value streams rather than departments. Each value stream had clear metrics for value delivery and the autonomy to use their resources as needed. They implemented rolling-wave budgeting with quarterly adjustments based on actual results and market conditions.

The transformation was remarkable. Within six months, they had:

- Reduced their burn rate by 40% while accelerating feature delivery
- Eliminated funding battles between departments
- Gained the ability to quickly fund new opportunities as they emerged
- Created clear visibility into which initiatives were actually generating value

The key insight wasn't about spending less - it was about spending smarter by funding value streams directly and giving teams the autonomy to optimize their resource usage.

In this chapter, we'll explore how to implement these modern financial practices in your startup. We'll cover everything from basic financial metrics to sophisticated value stream funding models. You'll learn how to:

- Structure your finances around value streams instead of departments
- Implement dynamic funding models that enable rapid adaptation
- Use participatory budgeting to engage teams in financial decisions
- Set up guardrails that enable autonomy while managing risk
- Create financial MVPs to test new initiatives safely

Whether you're a founder who breaks out in a cold sweat at the mention of financial statements, or a numbers whiz looking to modernize your financial strategy, this chapter will give you the tools to build a financial foundation that enables rather than constrains your growth.

Are you ready to unlock financial mastery and set your startup on the path to sustainable, value-driven growth? Let's dive in.

II. The Importance of Financial Management in Scaling

A. Why Financial Literacy is Crucial for Founders with a Value Stream Focus

As a founder, you might be tempted to delegate all financial matters to your CFO or accounting team. However, in a value stream-based organization, financial literacy takes on new importance. You need to understand not just traditional financial metrics, but how money flows through your value streams and enables value creation.

Financial literacy for modern founders means:

- Understanding value stream economics and how to measure value delivery
- Being able to make dynamic resource allocation decisions
- Knowing how to set up and adjust financial guardrails
- Making informed decisions about value stream funding

Here's why it's crucial:

1. **Strategic Decision Making:** Every major decision affects your value streams. Whether it's spinning up a new value stream, adjusting resource allocation, or investing in capabilities, understanding the financial implications helps you make better decisions.

2. **Investor Communications:** Modern investors increasingly understand value stream-based organizations. Being able to discuss your financials in terms of value streams and their performance will increase your credibility.
3. **Early Problem Detection:** Understanding value stream metrics helps you spot potential issues early. Is a value stream's cost exceeding its value delivery? Are resources misaligned with opportunities? These insights let you course-correct before problems become critical.
4. **Dynamic Resource Allocation:** Rather than getting locked into annual budgets, you need to understand how to reallocate resources dynamically based on value stream performance and market opportunities.
5. **Value-Based Investment:** Understanding how each value stream contributes to your overall business helps you make better investment decisions focused on actual value creation rather than departmental politics.

B. How Modern Financial Practices Support Rapid Growth

Many founders fear that sophisticated financial management will slow them down. In reality, value stream-based financial practices provide the foundation for sustainable, rapid growth.

Here's how:

1. **Efficient Capital Allocation:** By understanding which value streams generate the most value, you can allocate capital more effectively. This means you're investing in areas that will drive the most growth.
2. **Flexible Resource Management:** Value stream-based funding allows you to shift resources quickly as opportunities emerge. You're not locked into rigid departmental budgets.
3. **Rapid Experimentation:** Financial MVPs and clear

guardrails make it safe to experiment with new value streams or initiatives while managing risk.

4. **Clear Value Metrics:** Each value stream has clear metrics for value delivery, making it easier to identify and double down on what's working.
5. **Scalable Decision Making:** By setting clear financial guardrails, you empower value stream teams to make local decisions while maintaining fiscal responsibility.

C. The Link Between Value Stream Performance and Investor Confidence

In the world of startups, perception is often reality. Modern investors are increasingly sophisticated about value stream-based organizations and want to see:

1. **Clear Value Stream Economics:** Understanding the unit economics and performance metrics of each value stream.
2. **Dynamic Resource Allocation:** Evidence that you can quickly shift resources to capture opportunities.
3. **Efficient Operations:** Proof that your value streams are optimizing their resource usage.
4. **Growth Potential:** Clear paths to scaling successful value streams.
5. **Risk Management:** How you use financial guardrails to enable autonomy while managing risk.

D. Setting Up for Success

To implement these modern financial practices, you need:

1. **Clear Value Stream Identification:** Understanding what value streams exist in your business and how they create value.
2. **Financial Guardrails:** Setting clear boundaries within which value streams can operate autonomously.

3. **Measurement Systems:** Implementing ways to track value stream performance and economics.
4. **Dynamic Funding Mechanisms:** Creating processes for adjusting funding based on performance and opportunities.
5. **Participatory Practices:** Engaging teams in financial decisions that affect their value streams.

Remember: Financial management in a modern startup isn't about control - it's about enabling value creation while managing risk. As we move forward in this chapter, we'll explore exactly how to implement these practices in your startup, starting with the key metrics you need to track.

III. Lean Budgeting

As your startup scales, traditional annual budgeting becomes increasingly problematic. The practice of allocating fixed annual budgets to departments not only slows your ability to respond to market opportunities but can actually hinder innovation and value creation. This is where lean budgeting comes in - a modern approach that aligns funding with value streams and enables rapid adaptation to changing conditions.

Let me share a story that illustrates this perfectly. I recently worked with a fast-growing fintech startup that was struggling with their traditional budgeting process. Despite having a great product and strong market traction, they found themselves constantly fighting over resources between departments. Marketing needed more budget for growth initiatives, while product development was constrained by their annual allocation, unable to pursue promising opportunities that emerged mid-year. The engineering team was frustrated because they couldn't quickly reallocate resources to address technical debt that was slowing them down.

We helped them transition to a lean budgeting approach, and the transformation was remarkable. Within two quarters, they had:

- Reduced their decision-making cycle for new initiatives from months to days
- Improved their resource utilization by 40%
- Increased their speed-to-market for new features by 60%
- Significantly improved team morale by eliminating budget battles

Let's explore how you can implement lean budgeting in your startup.

A. Understanding the Lean Budgeting Mindset

Lean budgeting represents a fundamental shift in how we think about resource allocation:

Traditional Budgeting	Lean Budgeting
Annual Cycles Fixed yearly budgets	**Quarterly Reviews** Regular adjustments
Department-Based Siloed resources	**Value Stream-Based** Flow-based funding
Fixed Allocations Rigid distribution	**Dynamic Funding** Flexible reallocation
Detailed Controls Line-item oversight	**Guardrails** Boundary-based control
Top-Down Hierarchical decisions	**Participatory** Collaborative choices

The key principles of lean budgeting include:

1. Fund Value Streams, Not Departments
    - Allocate resources to customer value streams
    - Enable end-to-end value delivery
    - Break down departmental silos
2. Make Smaller, More Frequent Decisions
    - Move from annual to quarterly cycles
    - Enable rapid reallocation based on results
    - Reduce risk through smaller bets
3. Use Guardrails Instead of Detailed Controls
    - Set clear boundaries for decisions
    - Enable autonomous team decisions
    - Focus on outcomes rather than inputs
4. Measure Value Creation
    - Track value stream metrics
    - Monitor return on investment
    - Enable data-driven adjustments

B. Implementing Lean Budgeting

Here's a practical framework for implementing lean budgeting in your startup:

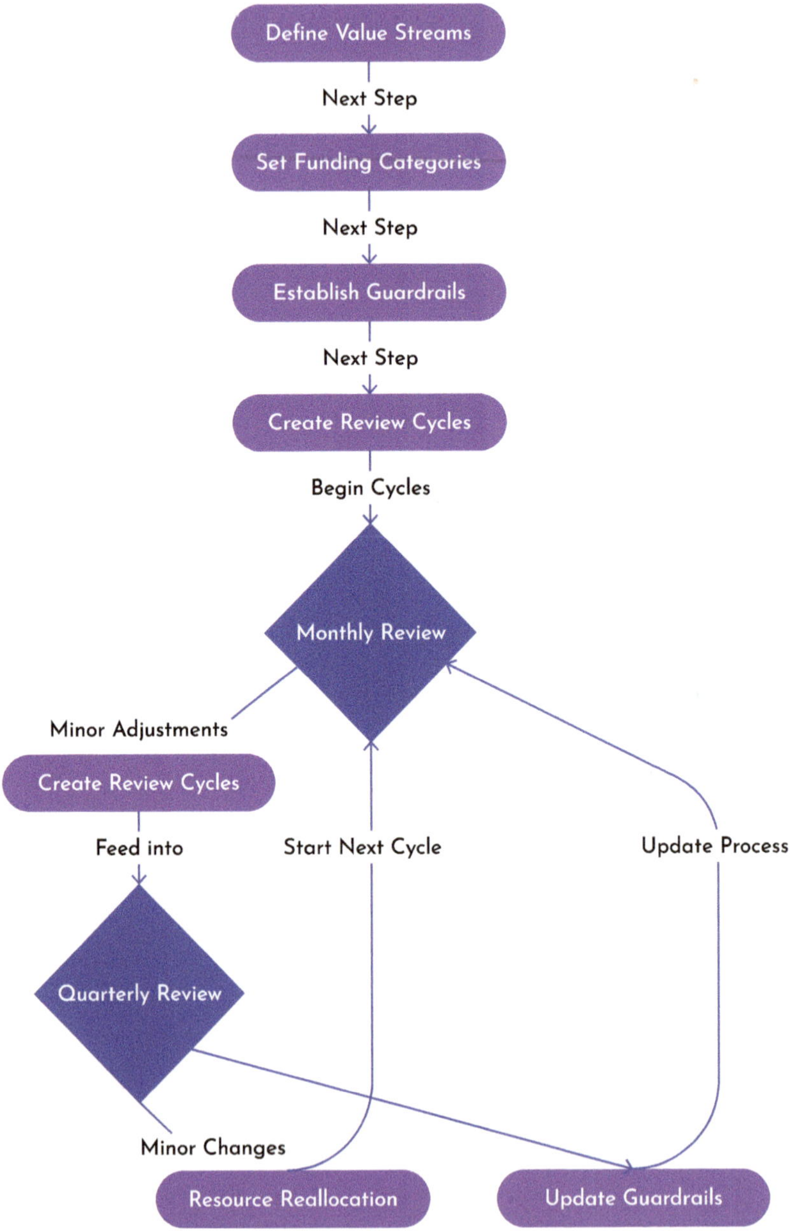
Define Value Streams
Next Step
Set Funding Categories
Next Step
Establish Guardrails
Next Step
Create Review Cycles
Begin Cycles
Monthly Review
Minor Adjustments
Create Review Cycles
Feed into
Start Next Cycle
Update Process
Quarterly Review
Minor Changes
Resource Reallocation
Update Guardrails

1. **Define Your Value Streams First, identify your key value streams - the end-to-end flows that deliver value to customers. These might include:**
    - Customer Acquisition Stream
    - Product Development Stream
    - Customer Success Stream
    - Platform Infrastructure Stream
2. **Set Up Funding Categories For each value stream, establish three types of funding:**
    - Operating Budget: Running current operations (70%)
    - Growth Budget: Scaling successful initiatives (20%)
    - nnovation Budget: Exploring new opportunities (10%)
3. **Establish Guardrails Create clear boundaries for decision-making:**
    - Financial thresholds for different decision levels
    - Key metrics that trigger reviews
    - Risk management parameters
    - Minimum and maximum allocations
4. **Create Review Cycles Implement regular review and adjustment processes:**
    - Monthly: Track metrics and make minor adjustments
    - Quarterly: Major allocation reviews and adjustments
    - Annual: Strategic review and guardrail updates

C. Participatory Allocation Process

One of the key innovations in lean budgeting is moving from top-down allocation to participatory decision-making. Here's how to implement this:

1. **Quarterly Planning**
    - Value stream leaders present plans and funding needs
    - Cross-functional teams review and provide input
    - Collaborative decisions on major allocations
    - Clear connection to strategic objectives
2. **Monthly Check-ins**
    - Review value stream metrics
    - Share learning and insights
    - Make minor adjustments as needed
    - Identify emerging opportunities
3. **Dynamic Reallocation**
    - Set clear triggers for reallocation
    - Enable fast movement of resources to opportunities
    - Learn from results and adjust quickly

D. Success Factors for Lean Budgeting

1. **Leadership Commitment**
    - Active executive sponsorship
    - Consistent communication
    - Role modeling new behaviors

2. **Clear Process Definition**
   - Well-documented procedures
   - Defined roles and responsibilities
   - Regular training and support
3. **Strong Metrics**
   - Clear value stream metrics
   - Regular measurement and reporting
   - Data-driven decisions
4. **Continuous Improvement**
   - Regular process reviews
   - Feedback incorporation
   - Ongoing refinement

By implementing lean budgeting, you create the financial flexibility needed to scale rapidly while maintaining appropriate control and governance. This approach aligns perfectly with value stream organization and enables rapid experimentation and innovation.

Most importantly, lean budgeting shifts your organization's focus from controlling costs to maximizing value creation - exactly what scaling startups need to succeed in today's fast-moving markets.

IV. Key Financial Metrics for Startups to Track

Understanding and tracking the right financial metrics is crucial for any startup looking to scale successfully. These metrics provide insights into your company's performance, help identify areas for improvement, and guide strategic decision-making.

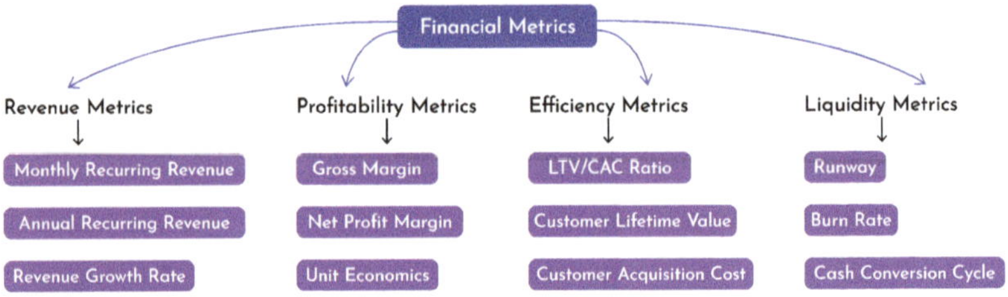

Let's dive into the essential metrics every startup should be tracking:

A. Revenue Metrics

1. **Monthly Recurring Revenue (MRR):** This is the predictable revenue your company can expect to receive every month. For SaaS and subscription-based businesses, this is a critical metric.

How to calculate: Sum of all monthly fees paid by your customers.

2. **Annual Recurring Revenue (ARR):** Similar to MRR, but on an annual basis. This gives a longer-term view of your predictable revenue.

How to calculate: MRR * 12

3. **Revenue Growth Rate:** This measures how quickly your revenue is increasing over time.

How to calculate: (Current Period Revenue - Prior Period Revenue) / Prior Period Revenue

B. Profitability Metrics

1. **Gross Margin:** This measures the percentage of revenue

left after accounting for the direct costs of producing your product or service.

How to calculate: (Revenue - Cost of Goods Sold) / Revenue

2. **Net Profit Margin:** This shows the percentage of revenue that translates into profit after all expenses are accounted for.

How to calculate: Net Income / Revenue

3. **Unit Economics:** This looks at the revenues and costs associated with a single unit of your product or service.

Key components:

- Average Revenue Per User (ARPU)
- Customer Acquisition Cost (CAC)
- Customer Lifetime Value (LTV)

C. Efficiency Metrics

1. **Customer Acquisition Cost (CAC):** This measures how much it costs to acquire a new customer.

How to calculate: Total Sales and Marketing Expenses / Number of New Customers Acquired

2. **Customer Lifetime Value (LTV):** This estimates the total revenue a business can expect from a single customer account throughout the business relationship.

How to calculate: (Average Revenue Per Account * Gross Margin %) / Churn Rate

3. LTV/CAC Ratio: This compares the lifetime value of a customer to the cost of acquiring that customer.

How to calculate: LTV / CAC

A healthy LTV/CAC ratio is generally considered to be 3:1 or higher.

D. Liquidity Metrics

How to calculate: Cash Balance at Beginning of Period - Cash Balance at End of Period

1. **Runway:** This estimates how long a company can continue operating before it runs out of cash, assuming current income and expense levels.

How to calculate: Cash Balance / Monthly Burn Rate

2. **Cash Conversion Cycle:** This measures how long it takes for a company to convert its investments in inventory and other resources into cash flows from sales.

How to calculate: Days Inventory Outstanding + Days Sales Outstanding - Days Payables Outstanding

E. The Importance of Context in Metric Analysis

While these metrics are crucial, they don't exist in a vacuum. In a lean budgeting environment, metrics must be analyzed both at the company level and within individual value streams. The key is understanding how these metrics interact across different contexts:

1. **Company-Level Context**
    - How metrics support overall business objectives
    - Industry benchmarks and competitive positioning
    - Market stage and growth expectations

2. **Value Stream Context**
    - How metrics inform resource allocation decisions
    - Value stream performance comparisons
    - Cross-stream dependencies and impacts
3. **Time-Based Context**
    - Metric trends over time
    - Seasonal variations
    - Growth stage considerations

For example, a high burn rate in one value stream isn't necessarily problematic if that stream is delivering proportionally higher value or building crucial capabilities. Similarly, varying efficiency metrics across value streams might be acceptable based on their different maturity levels and strategic importance.

When implementing lean budgeting, these metrics become crucial inputs for:

- Quarterly funding decisions
- Resource reallocation triggers
- Innovation investment choices
- Performance guardrail monitoring

The real power comes from tracking these metrics over time and understanding their implications for both individual value streams and the overall business. Are value streams becoming more efficient? Is resource allocation driving intended outcomes? These insights enable data-driven decisions about where to invest for maximum impact.

V. Strategies for Sustainable Profitability

While rapid growth is often the focus for startups, sustainable profitability across value streams is what will ensure your long-term success. In a lean budgeting environment, profitability strategies need to be both flexible and value-focused.

A. Value Stream-Based Pricing Strategies

Pricing becomes even more powerful when aligned with value streams. Here are key strategies to consider:

1. **Value Stream-Aligned Pricing**
   - Price based on value delivered by each stream
   - Consider cross-stream value propositions
   - Align pricing with value stream metrics
2. **Tiered Pricing by Value Stream**
   - Different pricing tiers within each value stream
   - Cross-stream bundling opportunities
   - Value-based upsell paths
3. **Dynamic Value-Based Pricing**
   - Adjust prices based on value stream performance
   - Use data from value stream metrics to inform pricing
   - Enable quick price experimentation and adjustment

B. Cost Management in a Value Stream Context

Cost management takes on new dimensions when viewed through a value stream lens:

1. **Value Stream Cost Optimization**
    - Track costs per value stream
    - Identify cross-stream efficiencies
    - Optimize resource sharing between streams
2. **Lean Resource Allocation**
    - Use quarterly funding reviews to optimize costs
    - Enable rapid reallocation to high-performing streams
    - Focus on value-driven cost decisions
3. **Automation and Efficiency**
    - Prioritize automation that enhances value delivery
    - Look for cross-stream automation opportunities
    - Focus on end-to-end process optimization

C. Balancing Growth Across Value Streams

The challenge becomes more nuanced when managing multiple value streams:

1. **Portfolio Approach**
    - Balance investment across value streams
    - Identify high-potential streams for growth investment
    - Maintain core streams while scaling new ones

2. **Value Stream Metrics**
   - Track profitability per value stream
   - Monitor cross-stream dependencies
   - Use data to inform resource allocation
3. **Growth Investment Criteria**
   - Clear metrics for value stream success
   - Defined triggers for increased investment
   - Regular review of value stream performance

D. Dynamic Forecasting and Scenario Planning

In a lean budgeting environment, forecasting becomes more dynamic:

1. **Value Stream Forecasting**
   - Project performance by value stream
   - Consider cross-stream impacts
   - Enable quick adjustments based on actual results
2. **Scenario Planning**
   - Develop scenarios at both company and value stream level
   - Plan for resource reallocation between streams
   - Consider cross-stream dependencies
3. **Regular Review Cycles**
   - Monthly value stream performance reviews

- Quarterly allocation adjustments
- Annual strategic portfolio review

Implementation Example: A B2B SaaS company reorganized their forecasting around value streams:

- **Customer Acquisition Stream:** Focus on CAC and conversion metrics
- **Product Development Stream:** Track feature adoption and usage
- **Customer Success Stream:** Monitor retention and expansion revenue
- **Infrastructure Stream:** Measure scalability and efficiency metrics

This enabled them to:

- Make faster resource allocation decisions
- Identify high-performing streams earlier
- Optimize cross-stream investments
- Improve overall profitability by 40%

By viewing profitability through a value stream lens and using lean budgeting principles, you create a more dynamic and responsive financial management system. This approach enables you to:

- Respond quickly to market opportunities
- Optimize resource allocation continuously
- Make data-driven investment decisions
- Maintain profitability while scaling

The key is maintaining the balance between short-term value stream performance and long-term sustainable growth. Regular reviews and adjustments, guided by clear metrics and guardrails, ensure that your pursuit of growth doesn't compromise long-term profitability.

VI. Funding Strategies for Different Stages of Growth

Securing the right funding at the right time is crucial for scaling your startup. However, the appropriate funding strategy can vary significantly depending on your stage of growth, business model, and market conditions. Let's explore the options:

A. Bootstrapping: When and How to Self-Fund

Bootstrapping means growing your business with little or no external funding. It's often the first stage for many startups and can continue to be a viable strategy even as you grow.

When to Consider:

- When you're just starting and validating your idea
- If you're in a business with low initial capital requirements
- If you want to maintain full control and ownership
- If your business can generate cash quickly

Strategies for Effective Bootstrapping:

1. **Focus on Revenue:** Prioritize getting paying customers as quickly as possible.
2. **Lean Operations:** Keep your costs as low as possible. Use

free tools, work remotely, and only hire when absolutely necessary.

3. **Reinvest Profits:** Put all early profits back into the business to fuel growth.

4. **Pre-sales and Crowdfunding:** Consider pre-selling your product or using crowdfunding platforms to generate initial capital.

B. Angel and Seed Funding: Navigating Early-Stage Investments

Angel and seed funding typically come into play when you've validated your idea and are looking to accelerate growth.

When to Consider:

- When you need capital to scale beyond what bootstrapping can provide
- If you're looking for not just money, but also expertise and networks
- When you're ready to give up some equity and control in exchange for growth

Strategies for Securing Angel and Seed Funding:

1. **Build Relationships:** Network in startup ecosystems, attend pitch events, and build relationships before you need the money.

2. **Perfect Your Pitch:** Develop a compelling story about your vision, traction, and potential.

3. **Understand Terms:** Familiarize yourself with term sheets and common deal structures.

4. **Consider Convertible Notes or SAFEs:** These can be

simpler and faster than priced equity rounds for early-stage startups.

5. **Look Beyond Money:** Choose investors who can provide valuable advice, connections, and support.

C. Venture Capital: Preparing for and Securing Larger Rounds

Venture capital comes into play when you're ready for significant scaling and can demonstrate strong growth potential.

When to Consider:

- When you have product-market fit and are ready to scale rapidly
- If you're in a market where speed to scale is crucial (e.g., winner-take-all markets)
- When you need significant capital for growth that other sources can't provide

Strategies for Venture Capital Funding:

1. Demonstrate Traction: VCs want to see strong growth metrics and market validation.
2. **Build a Strong Team:** VCs invest in teams as much as ideas. Ensure you have a balanced, experienced team.
3. **Know Your Numbers:** Be prepared to discuss detailed financial projections and unit economics.
4. **Understand VC Expectations:** VCs typically look for 10x returns. Ensure your growth potential aligns with these expectations.
5. **Choose the Right Partners:** Look for VCs who have

experience in your industry and can provide strategic value beyond just capital.

D. Alternative Funding Options

While bootstrapping, angel/seed funding, and VC are the most common paths, there are other options worth considering:

1. **Crowdfunding:** Platforms like Kickstarter or Indiegogo can be great for consumer products.
2. **Revenue-Based Financing:** You receive capital in exchange for a percentage of future revenue.
3. **Venture Debt:** Loans for VC-backed startups, often with warrants or rights to purchase equity.
4. **Strategic Partnerships:** Larger companies might provide funding in exchange for first rights to your technology or other strategic benefits.

E. Choosing the Right Funding Strategy

The key to a successful funding strategy is aligning it with your business model, growth stage, and long-term goals. Here are some factors to consider:

1. **Growth Rate:** If you're growing rapidly in a large market, VC might be appropriate. For steady, profitable growth, bootstrapping or alternative funding might be better.
2. **Capital Intensity:** Businesses requiring significant upfront investment (like hardware or biotech) may need to seek VC funding earlier, while software businesses might be able to bootstrap for longer.
3. **Market Opportunity:** If you're in a winner-take-all market,

you might need to prioritize rapid growth (and thus, larger funding rounds) over early profitability.

4. **Founder Goals:** Consider your personal goals. Are you aiming for a large exit, or do you want to build a sustainable business that you can run long-term? This will influence your funding choices.
5. **Control:** Remember that taking on investors means giving up some control. If maintaining full control is important to you, you might lean towards bootstrapping or revenue-based financing.
6. **Expertise Needs:** If you need more than just money – like industry expertise or important connections – angel or VC funding might be more attractive.

As you consider your funding strategy, here are some key questions to ask yourself:

1. **How capital intensive is my business?** Do I need significant upfront investment, or can I start generating revenue quickly?
2. **What's the competitive landscape like?** Am I in a winner-take-all market where rapid scaling is crucial?
3. **What are my personal goals as a founder?** Am I aiming for a large exit, or do I want to build a sustainable business I can run long-term?
4. **How predictable is my revenue?** Do I have the visibility to commit to revenue-based financing, or do I need the flexibility of equity financing?
5. **What's my risk tolerance?** Am I comfortable with the pressure and expectations that come with VC funding?
6. **Beyond capital, what other resources do I need?** Do I

need the expertise and connections that often come with angel or VC funding?

Remember, your funding strategy isn't set in stone. It's common for startups to bootstrap initially, then take on angel or seed funding as they start to scale, and potentially move to VC funding for larger growth rounds. The key is to make intentional choices at each stage that set your company up for long-term success.

VII. Financial Operations and Systems

As your startup scales, the robustness of your financial operations and systems becomes increasingly crucial - especially when implementing lean budgeting and value stream-based organization. While traditional financial systems focus on departmental control and annual cycles, modern startups need systems that can support dynamic resource allocation while maintaining appropriate oversight.

A. Setting up Value Stream-Aligned Financial Processes

The foundation of effective financial operations in a value stream organization starts with your chart of accounts. Rather than organizing purely by department or function, you need a structure that can track and support value stream performance. This means designing your accounts to capture both direct costs and shared resources across streams, while maintaining the visibility needed for lean budgeting decisions.

I recently worked with a scaling fintech startup that transformed their financial processes to support value streams. They struggled initially, trying to retrofit their traditional accounting structure to track value stream performance. The breakthrough came when they redesigned their chart of accounts from the ground up, starting with the question: "How does value flow through our organization?"

This led them to create a multi-dimensional structure that could track both functional costs (like engineering or marketing) and value stream attribution. The result was remarkable - they could now see not just how much they were spending, but how those expenditures contributed to value creation across different streams.

B. Choosing and Implementing Financial Software

Selecting the right financial software becomes more complex when supporting value streams and lean budgeting. Traditional accounting packages like QuickBooks or Xero can serve as your foundation, but they need to be augmented with capabilities that support dynamic resource allocation and value stream tracking.

The key is finding tools that can grow with your organization while supporting more frequent decision cycles. For example, a B2B SaaS company I advised started with QuickBooks Online but enhanced it with custom reporting layers that tracked value stream metrics. As they scaled, they migrated to NetSuite, implementing specialized modules for value stream management. This gradual evolution allowed them to maintain financial control while building the capabilities they needed for dynamic resource allocation.

When evaluating software, look beyond basic accounting features. Consider how the system will support your quarterly funding cycles, track performance against guardrails, and enable quick reallocation decisions. The goal is to create a financial technology stack that enables rather than constrains your value stream organization.

C. Enhanced Financial Reporting

Financial reporting in a value stream organization needs to go beyond traditional P&Ls and balance sheets. While these remain important, you also need visibility into value stream performance, resource utilization, and the effectiveness of your resource allocation decisions.

One startup I worked with developed a three-layer reporting approach. The foundation was traditional financial statements, providing the bedrock of financial control. The second layer tracked value stream performance, showing how resources translated into customer value. The top layer focused on resource allocation effectiveness, helping them optimize their quarterly funding decisions.

This comprehensive approach to reporting enabled them to maintain strong financial controls while supporting the dynamic decision-making needed in a scaling startup. They could quickly identify which value streams were performing well and needed additional investment, while maintaining clear visibility into overall financial health.

D. Building a Value Stream-Oriented Financial Team

The evolution of your financial team should match the maturity of your value stream organization. Rather than following the traditional progression from bookkeeper to CFO, consider how each role needs to adapt to support value streams and lean budgeting.

For instance, when hiring financial analysts, look for people who can partner effectively with value stream leaders. They need to understand not just the numbers, but how those numbers connect to value creation. Your controllers need to balance traditional accounting rigor with the flexibility required for dynamic resource allocation.

I saw this work particularly well at a rapidly growing marketplace startup. They embedded financial analysts directly in their major value streams, while maintaining a central finance team for core accounting and compliance. This hybrid structure gave them both the local expertise needed for value stream optimization and the central control required for sound financial management.

The key is building a team that can maintain financial discipline while enabling the speed and flexibility needed in a scaling startup. Look for people who understand both traditional financial principles and modern value stream concepts. They should be comfortable with more frequent planning cycles and able to support rapid decision-making while maintaining appropriate controls.

When it comes to timing these hires, let your value stream maturity be your guide. As streams become more established and complex, they'll need dedicated financial support. As your quarterly funding cycles become more sophisticated, you'll need people who can facilitate effective resource allocation decisions.

Remember, the goal of your financial operations is not just to track money, but to enable informed decisions that drive growth. By building systems and teams that support both value streams and lean budgeting, you create the foundation needed for sustainable scaling.

VIII. Exit Strategies and Financial Planning

While it may seem premature to think about exits when you're focused on growth, having a clear exit strategy can actually help guide your scaling efforts and ensure you're building long-term value. Let's explore key considerations for exit planning:

A. Types of Exit Strategies

There are several potential exit strategies for startups:

1. **Initial Public Offering (IPO):** Going public by offering shares to the public.
2. **Acquisition:** Being purchased by another company.
3. **Merger:** Combining with another company.
4. **Secondary Sale:** Selling a portion of shares to new investors while the company remains private.
5. **Management Buyout:** The management team purchases the business from current owners/investors.

Each of these has different implications for founders, employees, and investors.

B. Financial Preparations for Different Exit Scenarios

Regardless of your chosen exit strategy, certain financial preparations are crucial:

1. **Clean and Audited Financials:** Ensure your financial records are impeccable and can withstand scrutiny.
2. **Strong Financial Controls:** Implement robust financial processes and controls.
3. **Clear Growth Metrics:** Be able to demonstrate clear, sustainable growth trends.
4. **Efficient Operations:** Show that you've optimized your operations for profitability.
5. **Tax Planning:** Ensure your tax situation is optimized for a potential exit.

C. Valuation Considerations for Exits

Understanding how your company will be valued is crucial for exit planning. Key factors that can impact valuation include:

1. **Revenue Growth:** Consistent, strong growth is typically valued highly.
2. **Profitability:** While many startups prioritize growth over profitability, showing a clear path to profitability (or actual profitability) can significantly impact valuation.
3. **Market Size and Position:** Your total addressable market and your position within it are crucial.
4. **Customer Metrics:** Things like customer acquisition cost, lifetime value, and churn rate are important.
5. **Intellectual Property:** Strong IP can be a significant value driver.
6. **Team:** The strength and completeness of your management team can impact valuation.

Different industries and exit strategies may emphasize different factors. For example, SaaS companies are often valued based on a multiple of Annual Recurring Revenue (ARR), while e-commerce companies might be valued based on a multiple of EBITDA.

D. The Importance of Long-Term Financial Planning

Even if an exit isn't on your immediate horizon, long-term financial planning is crucial. This includes:

1. **Scenario Planning:** Model different growth trajectories and their financial implications.

2. **Capital Structure Planning:** Understand how different funding decisions will impact your long-term options.

3. **Reinvestment Strategy:** Plan how you'll allocate resources to fuel long-term growth.

4. **Succession Planning:** Ensure the business isn't overly dependent on any one person.

E. Balancing Short-Term Growth with Long-Term Value Creation

One of the biggest challenges for scaling startups is balancing the pressure for short-term growth with the need to build long-term value. Here are some strategies:

1. **Focus on Sustainable Growth:** Prioritize profitable growth over growth at all costs.

2. **Invest in Infrastructure:** Build scalable systems and processes that can support long-term growth.

3. **Develop Strong Unit Economics:** Ensure your fundamental business model is sound.

4. **Build Strategic Moats:** Invest in areas that will provide long-term competitive advantages.

5. **Align Incentives:** Ensure your team is incentivized for long-term value creation, not just short-term metrics.

Remember, the best exit strategy is to build a strong, valuable company. By focusing on sustainable growth, strong unit economics, and long-term value creation, you'll not only increase your chances of a successful exit but also build a more resilient company capable of weathering market uncertainties.

Blueprint Summary

Financial mastery in scaling startups centers on implementing lean budgeting and value stream-based financial management. This modern approach replaces traditional departmental budgeting with dynamic funding models that enable rapid adaptation while maintaining appropriate controls.

1. **Modern Financial Foundation**
    - Shift from traditional annual budgets to lean funding approaches
    - Implementation of value stream funding models
    - Establishment of financial guardrails for autonomous operation
    - Development of rapid response capabilities for market opportunities
    - Integration of risk management with financial flexibility
2. **Lean Budgeting Implementation**
    - Quarterly funding cycles replacing annual budgets
    - Participatory decision-making processes for resource allocation
    - Clear metrics and performance targets by value stream
    - Regular review and adjustment mechanisms
    - Systematic approach to resource reallocation
    - Balance between autonomy and control

3. **Value Stream Financial Management**
    - Direct resource allocation to value streams
    - Clear metrics for measuring value creation
    - Cross-stream synergy identification and optimization
    - Performance-based funding adjustments
    - Value-driven investment decisions
    - Integration of financial and operational metrics
4. **Metrics and Performance Management**
    - Comprehensive measurement systems for value streams
    - Real-time visibility into performance metrics
    - Regular review cycles for optimization
    - Multi-dimensional performance assessment
    - Integration of financial and operational metrics
    - Early warning systems for issues and opportunities
5. **Financial Operations Excellence**
    - Robust systems supporting dynamic allocation
    - Processes enabling rapid decision-making
    - Financial teams with value stream expertise
    - Integration of traditional and modern practices
    - Scalable operational infrastructure
    - Balance between control and flexibility

These elements work together to create an integrated system for modern financial management. Each component reinforces the others, enabling both rapid growth and sustainable operations. Success requires careful attention to all elements while maintaining flexibility to adapt to changing conditions.

Conclusion

The journey to financial mastery in scaling startups requires fundamental shifts in how we think about and manage resources. Traditional annual budgeting and departmental allocations must give way to more dynamic, value-focused approaches. The key is implementing lean budgeting practices that enable rapid adaptation while maintaining appropriate controls.

Success comes from creating clear links between funding and value creation through value stream-based financial management. This requires not just new processes, but new ways of thinking about resource allocation and performance measurement. The most successful startups treat financial management as a strategic capability that enables growth rather than a control function that constrains it.

The path forward begins with implementing lean budgeting practices, then gradually building more sophisticated capabilities around value stream management and performance optimization. Your financial systems and teams should evolve with your company, providing increasingly sophisticated support while maintaining the agility needed for rapid scaling.

This approach to financial management sets the stage for the organizational evolution we'll explore in Chapter 5. While lean budgeting and value stream funding provide the financial foundation for scaling, they require appropriate organizational structures to be truly effective. The marriage of modern financial practices with effective organizational design creates the framework needed for sustainable growth.

The transition to Chapter 5 is natural—because ultimately, your ability to implement lean budgeting and value stream funding depends heavily on your organizational structure. As we move from financial management to organizational design, you'll learn how to create structures that enable both efficient operations and rapid innovation while maintaining the financial discipline needed for sustainable scaling.

Chapter No. 5

EVOLUTION: Architect Your Empire

I. The Imperative of Organizational Evolution

In the dynamic world of startups, standing still is equivalent to moving backward. As your company grows from a small, scrappy team to a larger, more complex organization, the structures and processes that once served you well can quickly become obstacles to further growth. This is where the concept of organizational evolution becomes crucial.

Evolution, in the context of scaling startups, is not just about growing bigger - it's about growing smarter. It's about designing an organization that can adapt, learn, and continually improve as it scales. It's about creating a structure that empowers your team to execute on your vision efficiently and effectively, no matter how large you become.

But evolution is not without its challenges. As you scale, you'll face pressures to conform to traditional corporate structures. You'll be tempted to create departments and hierarchies that seem to promise order and control. Venture capitalists might push you to hire C-level executives for every function, believing this is what a "real" company looks like.

However, as I learned during a year-long project with a $2 billion company, these traditional structures can actually hinder growth and innovation. In that project, we faced the challenge of "de-scaling" - breaking a monolithic organization of 2000 engineers into 12 smaller, more agile startups. This experience taught me valuable lessons about how to structure organizations for sustainable growth and adaptability.

In this chapter, we'll explore a different approach - a Product Governance model that allows companies to scale without losing their agility or innovative spirit. We'll dive deep into the pillars of organizational evolution:

1. Translating Strategy into Action
2. Organizing Around Value Streams
3. Fostering Continuous Improvement
4. Building Communities of Practice
5. Validating Ideas Efficiently

This model isn't just theoretical - it's been battle-tested in both large corporations and fast-growing startups. It's designed to help you architect an empire that can grow without becoming bogged down by bureaucracy or losing sight of its mission.

So, are you ready to evolve? Let's dive in and explore how to build an organization that doesn't just get bigger, but gets better as it grows.

II. Translating Strategy into Action

One of the biggest challenges scaling startups face is maintaining alignment between long-term vision and day-to-day execution. As your team grows, it becomes increasingly difficult to ensure that everyone is working towards the same goals. This is where a structured strategy translation framework becomes invaluable.

Let's explore how to translate high-level strategy into actionable work through each level of the hierarchy:

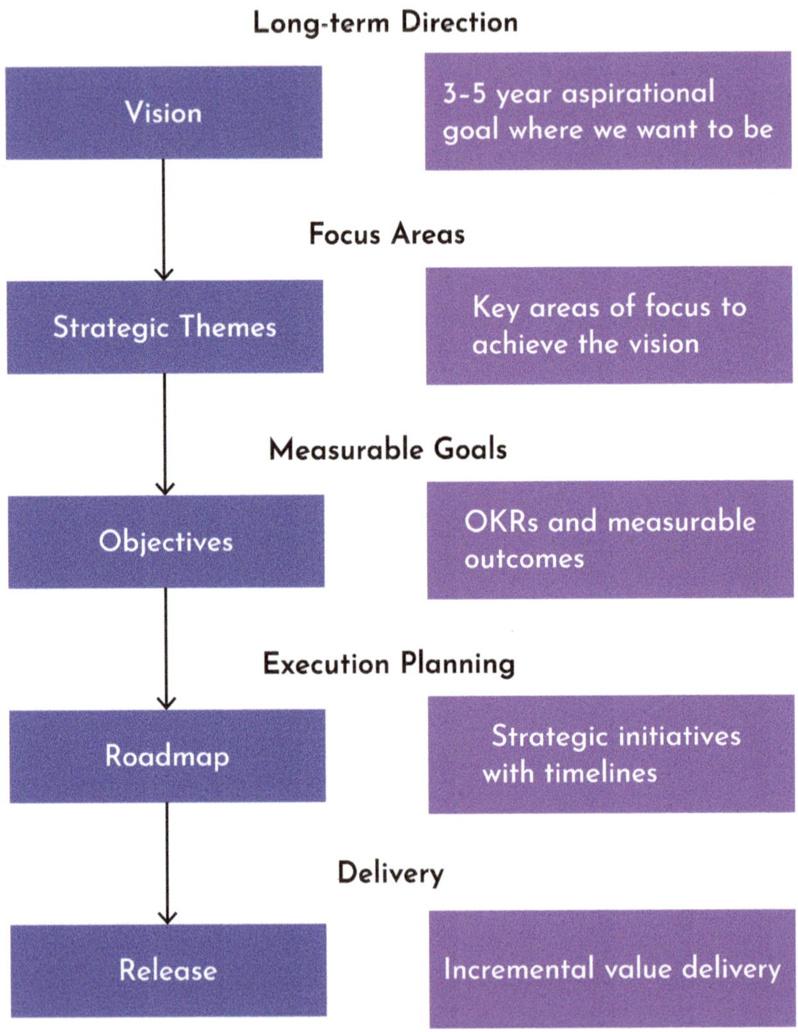

1. Start with Vision and Strategic Themes Your journey begins with your company's vision - your long-term aspirational goal. For example, let's say you're running

a fintech startup with the vision of “making investing accessible to everyone.” This vision informs your strategic themes, such as “Digital Financial Inclusion” and “User Education.”

2. Define Objectives through OKRs Based on your vision and strategic themes, define clear objectives using the OKR (Objectives and Key Results) framework. These should be ambitious, measurable, and time-bound. For our fintech startup, some OKRs might be:

   Objective (aligned with Digital Inclusion theme): Become the go-to investing app for millennials

   - **Key Result 1:** Increase our millennial user base from 100,000 to 500,000
   - **Key Result 2:** Achieve a 4.8 star rating on app stores with at least 50,000 reviews
   - **Key Result 3:** Increase average user session time from 5 minutes to 12 minutes

   Objective (aligned with User Education theme): Launch and grow our fractional stock trading feature

   - **Key Result 1:** Release fractional stock trading feature by end of Q2
   - **Key Result 2:** Achieve 100,000 users making at least one fractional trade per month by end of Q4
   - **Key Result 3:** Fractional trades to account for 30% of all trades on the platform by end of Q4

3. Create Your Roadmap Your roadmap organizes strategic initiatives into a coherent timeline. Each roadmap item should clearly support your objectives. For our fintech startup, the roadmap might include:

- **Q1:** Develop fractional stock trading infrastructure
- **Q2:** Launch fractional trading feature
- **Q3:** Implement personalized stock recommendations
- **Q4:** Roll out comprehensive user education platform

4. Plan Releases Through Prioritized Features Break down roadmap initiatives into specific features and prioritize them based on impact and dependencies. For the "fractional stock trading" initiative, prioritized features might include:
   - Core fractional trading engine
   - User interface for fractional orders
   - Real-time pricing system
   - Educational content and tutorials
   - Beta testing program
5. Create Development Stories Finally, transform prioritized features into detailed development stories that teams can execute in their sprints. For example, the "core fractional trading engine" might break down into:
   - Research regulatory requirements
   - Design database schema
   - Implement order processing system
   - Build reconciliation system
   - Create automated test suite
6. Regular Review and Adjustment While vision and strategic themes remain relatively stable, other elements should be reviewed and adjusted regularly:

- **Objectives (OKRs):** Quarterly review and reset
- **Roadmap:** Monthly adjustment based on progress and market changes
- **Features and Stories:** Bi-weekly refinement during sprint planning

This hierarchical approach ensures that every piece of work, from the smallest development task to the largest initiative, traces back to your company's vision. It provides the structure needed for scaling while maintaining the flexibility to adapt to changing circumstances.

For example, a developer working on the fractional trading database schema can see how their work connects to the feature, which supports the roadmap initiative, which achieves specific OKRs, which align with strategic themes, which ultimately serve the vision of making investing accessible to everyone.

Case Study: Strategy Alignment Through OKRs at a Traditional Bank In Portugal

I once worked with one of Portugal's largest banks that was struggling with the classic disconnect between IT teams and business strategy. For years, developers had been treated as mere executors of tasks, given strict deadlines without context, and had little understanding of how their work contributed to the bank's larger goals.

We implemented an OKR-driven approach that transformed this dynamic. Here's how it played out:

1. We started by bringing developers and executives together in the same room - something that had never happened before in the bank's history. The developers were initially surprised to be included in strategic

discussions, but this proved to be a crucial first step in breaking down traditional hierarchical barriers.

2. We defined company-level OKRs that bridged business and technical objectives. For the first time, developers weren't just receiving orders - they were part of the strategic conversation. They could ask questions, challenge assumptions, and provide technical insights that shaped the objectives.

3. What made this particularly powerful was that teams could design their own OKRs that aligned with company objectives. Instead of being handed down arbitrary deadlines, they could commit to what they knew was achievable within a quarter. This shift from push to pull created a new sense of ownership and responsibility.

4. The quarterly rhythm of OKRs also transformed the pace of work. Rather than constantly rushing to meet weekly or monthly deadlines, teams could plan and execute more thoughtfully within the quarter timeframe. This longer horizon allowed for better technical decisions and more sustainable pace of development.

5. We implemented a regular cadence of OKR reviews and planning sessions that kept everyone aligned while maintaining autonomy at the team level.

The results were transformative. For the first time in their careers, developers expressed that they truly understood how their work contributed to the bank's overall strategy. One senior developer remarked, "In my 15 years here, this is the first time I feel like I'm building something meaningful, not just completing tasks."

The impact went beyond just improved morale. Cross-functional collaboration increased significantly as teams could see how their work connected to other departments' objectives. Technical decisions became more strategic as developers could align architectural choices with business goals. The quality of work improved as teams took more ownership of outcomes rather than just outputs.

Most importantly, the bank saw faster progress toward its strategic goals because everyone was rowing in the same direction. Teams were no longer just going through the motions - they were actively engaged in achieving company objectives because they understood and believed in them.

This case study illustrates a crucial lesson for scaling startups: as you grow, maintaining alignment between strategy and execution becomes increasingly challenging. OKRs provide a framework that not only creates this alignment but also empowers teams by giving them autonomy within a clear strategic context. When people understand the "why" behind their work and have the freedom to determine the "how," they become truly invested in the company's success.

For startups that are scaling rapidly, this kind of alignment and autonomy is fundamental. It helps prevent the fragmentation that often comes with growth while ensuring everyone maintains sight of the north star. The Portuguese bank's experience shows that even in traditional, hierarchical organizations, OKRs can create a more empowered, aligned, and effective organization.

III. Organizing Around Value Streams

As startups scale, there's often pressure to adopt traditional corporate structures, with separate departments for functions like product, engineering, marketing, and sales. Many venture capitalists even push for this, seeing it as a sign of a "mature" company. This traditional approach extends beyond just organization - it typically includes departmental budgeting, where each function gets its annual allocation and operates in isolation.

However, this departmental structure can actually hinder growth and innovation. It creates silos, slows down decision-making, and disconnects teams from the end-to-end value they're creating for customers. Most importantly, it makes it impossible to truly understand and optimize the return on your investments, as value creation happens across departments, not within them.

A more effective approach for scaling startups is to organize around value streams, funded through lean budgeting practices and aligned via OKRs. A value stream is the series of steps required to deliver a product or service to the customer, from initial concept to delivery and support. By combining value streams with lean budgeting and OKRs, we create a system that optimizes for value creation rather than departmental efficiency.

Here's how to implement this integrated, value stream-based organization:

1. Identify Your Core Value Streams Start by identifying distinct product capabilities or services that could function as independent business units. Think of each value stream as a "mini-startup" that could potentially be its own business.

   For a SaaS company, these might include:

   - **Authentication Service:** A complete identity and access management system that could be sold as a standalone product
   - **Analytics Engine:** The data processing and visualization platform that could serve other businesses

- **Payment Processing System:** The complete billing and subscription management infrastructure
- **Integration Platform:** The API and integration framework that could be marketed independently
- **Customer Success Platform:** The onboarding, support, and customer engagement system

Each value stream should:

- Have its own clear value proposition
- Serve a specific market need
- Generate measurable business value
- Be capable of operating with relative independence
- Have potential to exist as a standalone product/service

2. Implement Value Stream Funding Instead of traditional departmental budgeting, implement a lean budgeting approach that funds value streams based on their OKRs:
    - **Quarterly Funding Cycles:** Replace annual departmental budgets with quarterly value stream funding
    - **OKR-Based Allocation:** Tie funding directly to specific objectives and key results
    - **Dynamic Reallocation:** Enable rapid reallocation of resources based on performance
    - **Autonomous Management:** Let value stream teams manage their own resources
    - **Results-Based Accountability:** Measure success by OKR achievement, not budget compliance

3. Create Cross-Functional Teams For each value stream, create a dedicated cross-functional team that includes all the skills needed to deliver value:
    - Product managers, developers, designers
    - Marketing and sales capabilities
    - Customer support expertise
    - Data and analytics skills
    - Operations and infrastructure knowledge
4. Establish Value Stream OKRs Each value stream needs clear objectives that:
    - Align with company-level OKRs
    - Focus on specific value delivery
    - Include measurable results
    - Guide funding decisions
    - Enable autonomous operation
5. Implement Lean Management Practices Support value stream operations with:
    - Visual management boards
    - Daily stand-ups
    - Continuous improvement practices
    - Regular OKR reviews
    - Dynamic funding adjustments

Let's visualize how this organizational approach works:

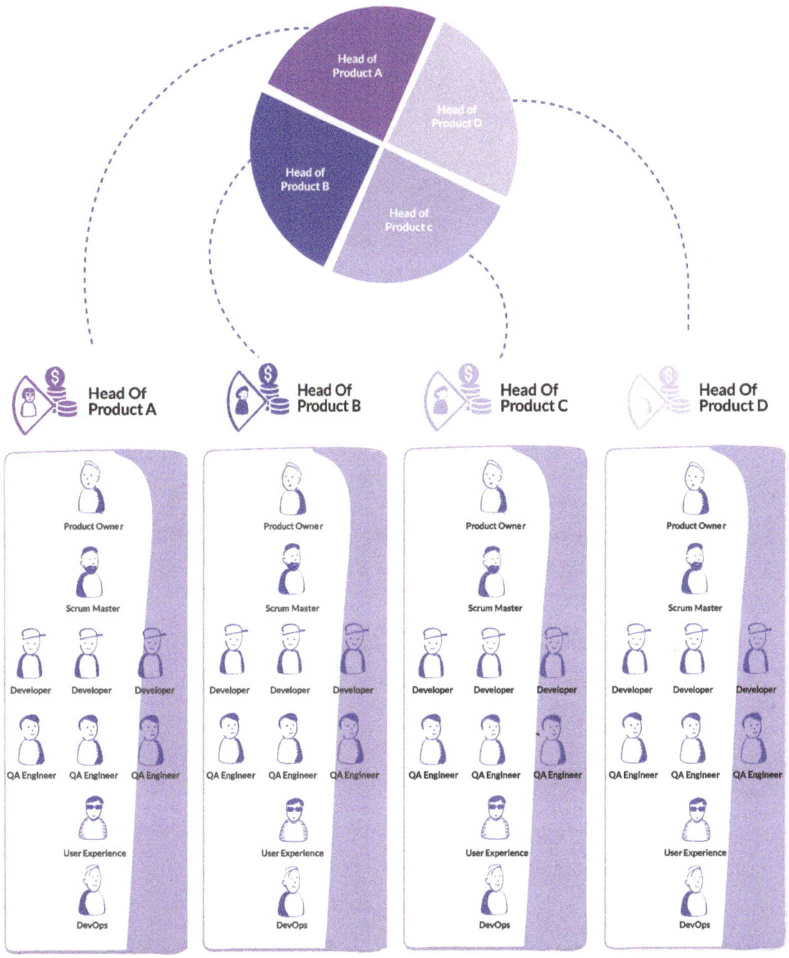

In this visualization, we see how different value streams operate independently while serving the overall company mission. Each stream contains all the capabilities needed to deliver value to customers - from product development to customer support. This autonomous structure enables:

- Faster decision-making within each value stream
- Clear ownership and accountability

- Reduced dependencies between teams
- Accelerated value delivery to customers
- Greater ability to scale individual streams based on demand

Notice how each value stream maintains its own complete set of capabilities while sharing common infrastructure and knowledge across streams. This balance between autonomy and alignment is key to successful scaling.

Case Study: Building ZapZap Through Independent Value Streams

I'm currently building ZapZap, a comprehensive business management platform, using this integrated approach of value streams, OKRs, and lean budgeting. Instead of organizing around traditional departments, we've structured the platform around four distinct value streams, each operating as an independent business unit with its own funding and OKRs:

1. **Business Dashboards Value Stream**
    - **Value Proposition:** Complete analytics and visualization product
    - **Team:** Data engineers, visualization specialists, UX experts
    - **Key OKRs:** User engagement, data processing efficiency
    - **Funding:** Tied directly to OKR achievement
2. **Strategic Planning Value Stream**
    - **Value Proposition:** Standalone strategic management product

- **Team:** Strategy experts, product designers, developers
- **Key OKRs:** Customer adoption, strategy execution metrics
- **Funding:** Based on quarterly objective completion

3. **Operational Roadmaps Value Stream**
    - **Value Proposition:** Product and portfolio management solution
    - **Team:** Product managers, UX designers, engineers
    - **Key OKRs:** Feature utilization, customer satisfaction
    - **Funding:** Aligned with roadmap delivery milestones
4. **Team Kanbans Value Stream**
    - **Value Proposition:** Team collaboration and task management
    - **Team:** Collaboration experts, UX specialists, developers
    - **Key OKRs:** Team adoption, workflow efficiency
    - **Funding:** Tied to usage and satisfaction metrics

The Power of Integration

What makes this approach particularly powerful is how the three elements - value streams, OKRs, and lean budgeting - work together:

- Value streams provide the organizational structure
- OKRs provide the alignment and direction
- Lean budgeting provides the resource allocation mechanism

This integration has enabled us to:

- Make faster decisions about resource allocation
- Track return on investment more accurately
- Foster entrepreneurial thinking within teams
- Scale different components at different rates
- Maintain strategic alignment while enabling autonomy

Results and Impact

This structure has delivered significant benefits:

- Clear ownership and accountability
- Rapid innovation within value streams
- Efficient resource utilization
- Strong strategic alignment
- Flexibility to evolve and scale

The lesson for other startups is clear: by integrating value streams, OKRs, and lean budgeting, you create a system that optimizes for value creation while maintaining strategic alignment. This approach not only makes your organization more scalable but also creates multiple paths for future growth and innovation.

Remember, this isn't just an organizational structure - it's a complete system for turning strategy into value through the efficient allocation of resources to the right opportunities. When these three elements work together effectively, you create an organization capable of sustained, profitable growth.

IV. Fostering Continuous Improvement

In a rapidly scaling startup, the ability to identify and address organizational challenges quickly is crucial. This is where the concept of an Organizational Impediment Board comes in.

An Organizational Impediment Board is a visual tool that helps teams and leaders identify, prioritize, and address obstacles that are hindering performance or growth. It's a key component of creating a culture of continuous improvement.

The Organizational Impediment Board provides a clear, visual way to identify, prioritize, and address obstacles to performance and growth. Here's how it's structured:

This board makes organizational improvement tangible and actionable. The columns show the progression of impediments from identification through resolution.

Here's how to implement an Organizational Impediment Board:

1. **Create the Board**

   Set up a physical or digital board with columns for:

   - Identified Impediments
   - Under Analysis
   - In Progress
   - Resolved

2. **Encourage Broad Participation**

   Make it easy for anyone in the organization to add impediments to the board. This could be through a physical board in a common area, a digital tool, or both.

3. **Regular Review Sessions**

   Hold weekly or bi-weekly sessions to review the board. These sessions should include representatives from different parts of the organization.

4. **Prioritize Impediments**

   Not all impediments are equal. Use a simple prioritization method (like impact vs. effort) to decide which impediments to tackle first.

5. **Assign Ownership**

   For each impediment you decide to address, assign a clear owner who will be responsible for driving the resolution.

6. **Track Progress**

   Regularly update the status of impediments on the board. Celebrate when impediments are resolved.

7. **Learn and Iterate**

   Use resolved impediments as learning opportunities. What systemic issues did they reveal? How can you prevent similar impediments in the future?

Case Study: Making Organizational Improvement Visible and Fun

Back in 2015, I had the privilege of working with one of the best companies I've encountered in my career - a vacation package booking company that had almost everything right. However, one challenge persisted: we lacked a systematic way to identify and address organizational problems.

The solution we implemented was both effective and memorable. We installed an Organizational Impediment Board right at the company's entrance - a location impossible to miss. What made this particularly powerful was our CEO's enthusiastic support for building a continuous improvement culture. He understood that making problems visible was the first step to solving them.

To add some personality to the initiative, my colleagues and I put up a Chuck Norris picture next to the board with the caption: "No organizational issue will resist me!" This touch of humor helped make the serious business of organizational improvement more approachable and engaging. Every employee who walked through the doors would see not only the current organizational challenges but also Chuck Norris's determined face promising to tackle them.

The process was simple but powerful: Every two weeks, we would bring together people from different levels of the organization - from executives to front-line employees - to discuss the issues posted on the board. This cross-hierarchical participation was crucial; it meant that everyone's voice could be heard, regardless of their position in the company.

During these sessions, we would:

1. Review existing impediments

2. Discuss new issues that had been posted
3. Assign clear ownership for addressing each problem
4. Track progress on previously identified issues
5. Celebrate resolved impediments

The beauty of this approach was its transparency and inclusivity. Anyone could post an organizational issue, and everyone could see what problems were being tackled. The board became a physical manifestation of our commitment to continuous improvement.

The Chuck Norris theme became a running joke that actually helped make the process more effective. People would say things like "Let's Chuck Norris this problem!" when taking on particularly challenging issues. It made addressing organizational problems feel less daunting and more like a shared mission.

This approach of combining serious organizational improvement with a touch of humor and pop culture proved remarkably effective at building a culture where identifying and solving organizational problems became part of everyone's daily work. Little by little, we were able to eliminate organizational obstacles and improve company operations while maintaining a positive, engaging atmosphere.

The lesson here is powerful: Sometimes the most effective organizational changes combine serious purpose with a touch of fun and personality. By making the impediment board both highly visible and slightly irreverent, we created a tool that not only helped solve problems but also reinforced our culture of continuous improvement in a way that engaged everyone in the company.

Today, whenever I implement organizational improvement

processes, I remember the Chuck Norris board and how it demonstrated that serious organizational transformation doesn't have to feel heavy or bureaucratic - it can be visible, inclusive, and even fun while still delivering significant results.

For scaling startups, this approach is absolutely crucial. When you're growing rapidly from 10 to 50 to 200 people, it's dangerously easy to lose the transparency and quick problem-solving ability that made you successful in the first place.

By implementing a visible, engaging impediment board early - and making it part of your culture through elements like our Chuck Norris theme - you create a lightweight but powerful mechanism to catch and fix organizational issues before they become growth-killing problems.

The beauty is in its simplicity: no expensive consultants, no complex frameworks, just a visible board, regular discussions, and a commitment to continuous improvement that scales naturally with your startup.

V. Building Communities of Practice

As your startup scales, maintaining and spreading expertise becomes increasingly challenging. Silos can form, best practices may not be shared, and innovations can remain isolated. Communities of Practice (CoPs) are a powerful tool to address these challenges.

A Community of Practice is a group of people who share a concern or a passion for something they do, and learn how to do it better as they interact regularly. In a startup context, CoPs can be centered around specific technologies, methodologies, or business functions.

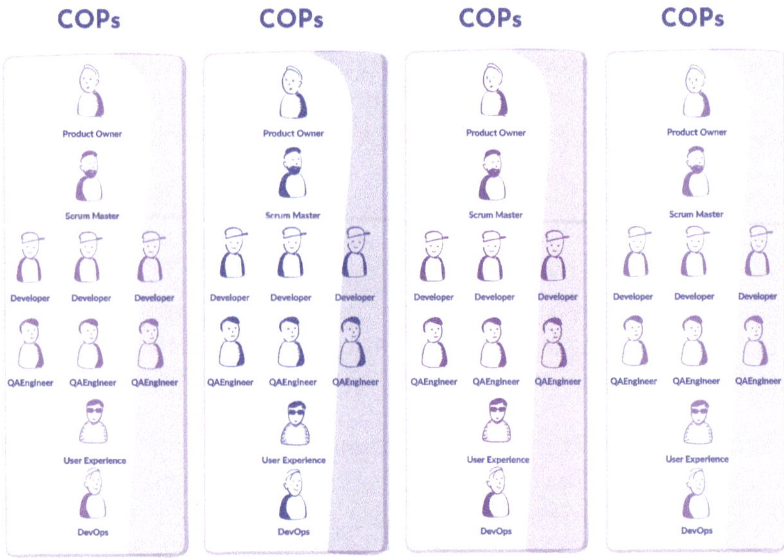

The visualization shows how different Communities of Practice operate as interconnected networks of expertise. Each community focuses on specific domains - technical, product, process, etc. - while maintaining connections with other communities. This structure:

- Facilitates knowledge sharing across teams
- Accelerates learning and innovation
- Creates career growth opportunities
- Maintains high standards of excellence
- Breaks down silos between departments

Notice how CoPs cut across organizational boundaries, creating valuable connections that wouldn't exist in traditional hierarchical structures.

Here's how to establish effective Communities of Practice:

1. **Identify Areas for CoPs**

   Look for areas where shared learning would be valuable. Common areas for CoPs in startups include:

- Frontend Development
- Data Science and Analytics
- User Experience Design
- Agile Methodologies
- Customer Success

2. **Find Champions**

   Identify passionate individuals who can lead each CoP. These champions should be knowledgeable in their area and excited about sharing and learning.

3. **Define the CoP's Purpose**

   Each CoP should have a clear purpose. This might include:

   - Sharing best practices
   - Solving common problems
   - Innovating in their domain
   - Mentoring and skill development
   - Standardizing practices across the organization

4. **Establish Regular Meetings**

   Set up recurring meetings for each CoP. These could be weekly, bi-weekly, or monthly, depending on the needs of the group.

5. **Create Sharing Platforms**

   Provide platforms for CoP members to share knowledge outside of meetings. This could be a Slack channel, a wiki, or a shared document repository.

6. **Encourage Cross-Pollination**

   While CoPs are domain-specific, encourage members to occasionally visit other CoPs. This can spark innovation through cross-disciplinary insights.

7. **Measure and Communicate Value**

   Regularly assess the impact of CoPs and communicate their value to the broader organization. This could include innovations developed, problems solved, or efficiency improvements.

Case Study: Building Excellence Through Communities of Practice

Continuing with the holiday booking company from 2015, we established several powerful Communities of Practice (CoPs) that transformed how we shared knowledge and drove excellence across the organization.

We created three key CoPs:

1. **Scrum Masters CoP:** This group took an innovative approach - they collaboratively created a roadmap of what the "perfect agile organization" would look like, then used their regular meetings to share experiences and solve problems on the journey toward that ideal. They would discuss real challenges they faced and collectively brainstorm solutions.

2. **Product Owners CoP:** Similarly, the Product Owners created their own vision of excellence and used their community to share challenges and victories in product development and stakeholder management.

3. **Technical Excellence CoP:** This group focused on elevating our engineering practices across all teams.

What made this particularly powerful was how we shared the knowledge. We started hosting "Pizza & Learnings" sessions where insights from these CoPs were shared with the wider organization.

These lunch sessions were recorded, and the best ones became part of our onboarding process for new hires. Imagine joining a company and being able to learn from dozens of real-world experiences shared by your future colleagues over pizza!

The results were transformative - this organic, social approach to knowledge sharing created a powerful learning culture that could scale with the organization. For any startup scaling rapidly, this combination of structured CoPs and informal knowledge sharing through recorded pizza sessions provides a blueprint for maintaining excellence while growing fast.

Remember, CoPs should be organic and driven by their members' needs and interests. As a leader, your role is to provide support and remove obstacles, not to dictate the CoP's activities.

VI. Validating Ideas Efficiently

In a rapidly evolving market, the ability to quickly validate new ideas is crucial. But how do we decide which ideas should move from discovery into actual development? This is where Design Sprints become invaluable. Popularized by Google Ventures, a Design Sprint is a time-constrained, five-phase process that serves as a critical bridge between your discovery and delivery tracks.

While we'll explore the complete Dual Track Development approach in the Product chapter, it's important to understand how Design Sprints fit into this larger picture. Your discovery track continuously researches and generates new ideas, while your delivery track (which we explored in Chapter 2 – Continous Delivery and Chapter 3 - Agility) focuses on building validated solutions.

Design Sprints serve as the validation mechanism between these two tracks, helping you decide which ideas are worth moving into development.

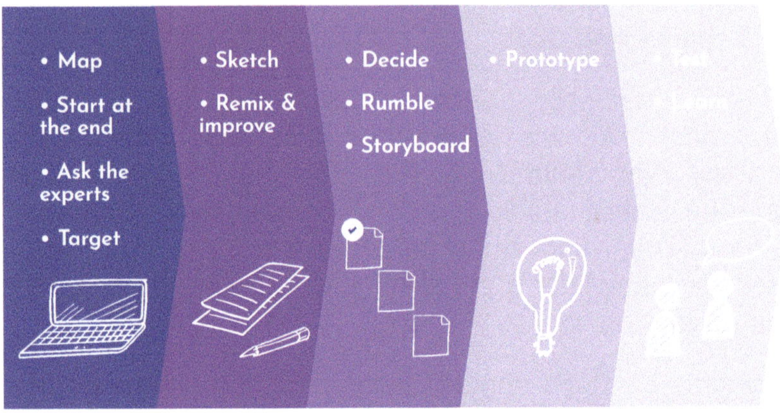

Here's how to implement Design Sprints as part of your discovery-to-delivery pipeline:

1. Understand the Design Sprint's Role in Dual Track Development A Design Sprint serves three critical functions:

    - Validates discoveries before committing development resources

    - Provides a structured way to test hypotheses from your discovery track

    - Creates a clear decision point for moving ideas into the delivery track

2. The Design Sprint Process A typical Design Sprint consists of five phases that bridge discovery and delivery:

- **Understand:** Synthesize insights from your discovery track
- **Sketch:** Transform research into potential solutions
- **Decide:** Choose which solution to validate
- **Prototype:** Create a realistic prototype for testing
- **Test:** Get feedback to inform the delivery track

3. Identify Sprint-Worthy Opportunities Not every idea from your discovery track needs a full Design Sprint. Look for opportunities that:
    - Have strong evidence from discovery research
    - Could significantly impact your key metrics
    - Would require substantial development investment
    - Need validation before committing delivery resources
    - Have unclear implementation requirements
4. Assemble the Right Team Include representatives from both discovery and delivery tracks:
    - **Discovery Track:** Researchers, designers, product managers
    - **Delivery Track:** Engineers, technical architects
    - **Facilitator:** Manages the process and bridges both tracks
    - **Decider:** Makes final go/no-go decisions about moving to delivery
5. Structure the Sprint for Decision-Making The goal is to make clear decisions about moving ideas to delivery:

- **Day 1:** Review discovery findings and align on the challenge
- **Day 2-3:** Develop and select potential solutions
- **Day 4:** Create prototype for validation
- **Day 5:** Test and make delivery decisions

Case Study: How a Simple Design Sprint Generated €500K Annual Revenue

While working with a holiday booking company, we used Design Sprints as the bridge between our discovery and delivery tracks. Our discovery track had identified a significant problem through user research: customers browsing vacation packages on mobile couldn't easily continue their search on desktop later.

Instead of immediately moving this into development, we ran a Design Sprint to validate potential solutions:

Day 1: We reviewed all the discovery research, including:

- User journey maps showing the mobile-to-desktop transition
- Analytics data on abandoned searches
- Customer support tickets about lost packages

Day 2-3: The team explored various solutions:

- Cross-device synchronization
- Account-based favorites
- Email-based package sharing
- Browser-based persistence

Day 4: We prototyped the simplest solution: an "email this package" button

Day 5: User testing revealed this simple solution resonated strongly with users

The Results:

- **Discovery Validated:** Confirmed the problem was worth solving
- **Solution Simplified:** Avoided over-engineering the solution
- **Clear Delivery Path:** Development team had precise requirements
- **Measurable Impact:** €500,000 additional annual revenue
- **Rapid Implementation:** Solution deployed within two weeks

This case study demonstrates the power of Design Sprints as a bridge between discovery and delivery. Without this structured validation process, we might have jumped straight from discovery into building a complex cross-device synchronization system. Instead, we found a simple solution that could be quickly delivered and immediately generate value.

Making the Bridge to Product Development

As we'll explore in detail in Chapter 7: PRODUCT, this approach of using Design Sprints to bridge discovery and delivery is part of a larger Dual Track Development methodology. The discovery track continuously researches and identifies opportunities, Design Sprints validate the most promising ones, and the delivery track (covered in Chapter 2 – Continous Delivery and Chapter 3 - Agility) builds the validated solutions.

This systematic approach ensures that:

- Discovery insights don't get lost in translation

- Development resources are focused on validated solutions
- Teams maintain a healthy balance between innovation and execution
- There's a clear process for moving from ideas to implementation
- Risk is reduced through validation before commitment

Remember, the goal isn't just to run successful Design Sprints—it's to create a reliable bridge between your discovery and delivery tracks, ensuring that your organization can consistently turn promising ideas into valuable features.

VII. Putting It All Together

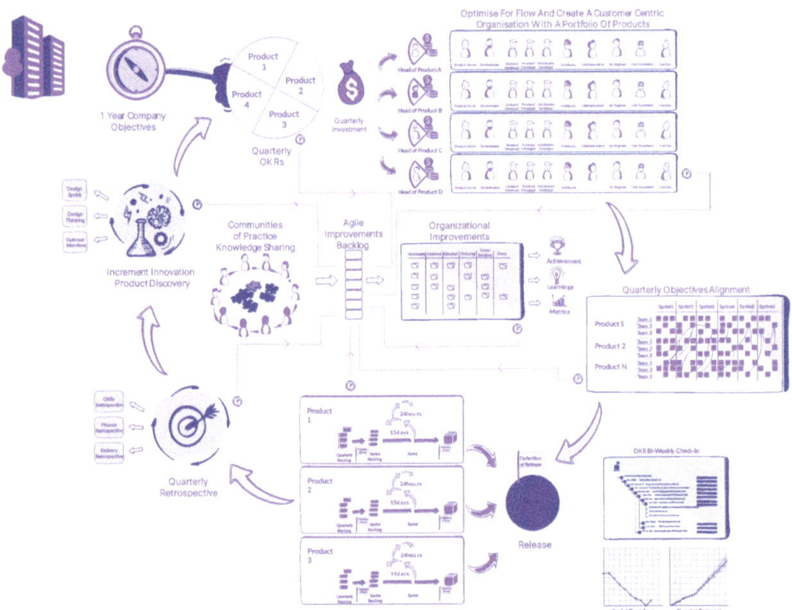

Now that we've explored each component of the Product Governance Framework, let's look at how they all fit together to create a cohesive system for scaling your startup.

1. **Strategy Translation**

   At the top level, we have the company strategy, which is translated into OKRs. These OKRs cascade down to inform the product roadmap and backlog. This ensures that every task your teams are working on is aligned with your overall strategic goals.

2. **Value Stream Organization**

   Instead of traditional departmental silos, your organization is structured around value streams. Each value stream team is cross-functional and empowered to deliver end-to-end value to customers.

3. **Continuous Improvement**

   The Organizational Impediment Board provides a mechanism for continuously identifying and addressing obstacles to performance and growth. This creates a culture of ongoing optimization and adaptation.

4. **Knowledge Sharing**

   Communities of Practice foster cross-team learning and innovation. They ensure that expertise is spread throughout the organization and that best practices are continually evolving.

5. **Idea Validation**

   Design Sprints provide a structured process for rapidly testing and validating new ideas. This allows you to innovate quickly while minimizing the risk of investing in ideas that won't resonate with customers.

Here's how these components work together in practice:

- The company sets its strategy and OKRs for the quarter.
- Value stream teams translate these OKRs into their product backlogs.

- As teams work through their backlogs, they use the Impediment Board to identify and address obstacles.
- Communities of Practice provide forums for sharing knowledge and solving common problems across teams.
- When significant new ideas or pivots are proposed, Design Sprints are used to rapidly validate them before committing to full development.

This integrated framework provides the structure needed to scale effectively while maintaining the agility and innovation that are crucial for startup success.

Blueprint Summary

Organizational evolution is about building structures and systems that enable rather than inhibit growth. This chapter focuses on creating scalable organizational designs that maintain startup agility while adding necessary structure. It's about evolving from a collection of individuals to a high-performing organization without losing the innovation and speed that drove early success.

1. **Organizational Design**
    - Value Stream Organization aligns teams and resources around key value delivery flows
    - Decision-Making Frameworks provide clear processes for strategic and operational decisions
    - Communication Structures ensure efficient information flow throughout organization
    - Authority Distribution balances autonomy with coordination needs

- Cross-functional Alignment ensures different parts work together toward common goals

2. **Governance Systems**
   - OKR Implementation connects strategy to execution, ensuring aligned goals
   - Strategic Planning Process creates structured approaches to setting/executing strategy
   - Portfolio Management enables effective prioritization across initiatives
   - Resource Allocation ensures limited resources go to highest-impact opportunities
   - Performance Monitoring provides visibility into execution and enables course correction

3. **Scaling Mechanisms**
   - Growth Phase Management helps navigate different organizational evolution stages
   - Team Structure Evolution ensures organization adapts to growing complexity
   - Process Scalability focuses on creating processes that work at larger scale
   - Knowledge Management maintains critical information as organization grows
   - Change Management enables evolution while maintaining stability

4. **Innovation Systems**
   - Communities of Practice bring together people to advance organizational capabilities
   - Innovation Frameworks provide structured approaches to generating new ideas

- Experimentation Processes enable systematic testing of new concepts
- Learning Organizations create environments for continuous improvement
- Knowledge Sharing ensures insights spread effectively throughout organization

5. **Culture Evolution**
   - Values Alignment ensures core values remain strong while adapting to scale
   - Behavioral Norms establish clear expectations for working together
   - Cultural Scalability focuses on maintaining cultural strength through growth
   - Leadership Development builds capability needed at each growth stage
   - Organizational Learning enables continuous improvement based on experience

Conclusion

The evolution of your organizational structure represents a critical transition in your scaling journey. It's about creating systems and structures that enable rather than constrain growth. The most successful startups understand that organizational design isn't about adding bureaucracy—it's about building frameworks that allow for coordinated action at scale while preserving the agility and innovation that drove early success.

Your organizational evolution must be intentional and progressive, starting with fundamental elements like clear value streams and basic governance, then building toward more sophisticated systems for innovation and scale. The key is to create structures that provide enough framework to enable efficient operation while maintaining the flexibility needed for rapid adaptation.

However, even the best organizational structure can only succeed with the right people in place. This brings us to Chapter 6: UPGRADE, where we'll explore how to attract, develop, and retain the talent needed to power your evolving organization. While organizational design provides the framework, it's the people within that framework who ultimately determine your success.

In the next chapter, we'll dive into creating comprehensive talent management systems that ensure you have the right people in the right roles as you scale. We'll see how combining effective organizational design with strong talent management creates the foundation for sustainable growth. The synergy between structure and talent enables your startup to scale efficiently while maintaining its innovative edge.

The transition from organizational design to talent management is natural—because ultimately, your organizational structure exists to enable your people to perform at their best. As we move from building the framework to filling it with exceptional talent, you'll learn how to create systems that attract and retain the people who will drive your company's continued success.

Chapter No. 6

UPGRADE: Attract and Retain Superstar Talent

I. The Talent Imperative in Scaling Startups

In the exhilarating world of startups, the art of building a team transcends mere recruitment. It's about curating a group of individuals who not only possess the skills to drive your company forward but also embody its aspirations and vision for the future. As a founder, your ability to attract, develop, and retain top talent will be one of the most critical factors in your startup's journey from promising newcomer to industry unicorn.

The challenge of building a stellar team is intensified in today's competitive talent market. The rise of remote work has expanded the talent pool globally, but it has also increased competition for the best and brightest. Today's workforce, particularly in the tech industry, is not just looking for a paycheck – they're seeking meaningful work, opportunities for growth, and a culture that aligns with their values.

Building a world-class team is one of the most crucial

challenges founders face when navigating the complex waters of talent management. Success in this area requires more than just basic hiring practices - it demands a comprehensive approach to building a team that can scale with your startup, adapt to challenges, and drive innovation.

The journey of building an exceptional team encompasses several critical elements that work together harmoniously:

- Understanding and defining your unique talent needs and company culture
- Strategically identifying and attracting top talent in a competitive market
- Creating excitement about your company's vision and the opportunities you offer
- Ensuring strong alignment between candidates and your organization
- Supporting continuous growth and development after hiring

In this chapter, we'll explore each of these essential aspects in depth, providing practical strategies, real-world examples, and actionable steps you can take to build a world-class team. We'll also address common challenges in talent management for scaling startups and provide insights on how to overcome them.

Remember, as a founder, your role in talent management goes beyond simply filling positions. You're the architect of your company's future, and every hire is a brushstroke on the masterpiece you're creating. With the right approach to talent management, you'll be equipped to not just hire employees, but to build a team of superstars who will help write the next chapters of your startup's success story.

Success in today's competitive landscape requires a holistic view of talent management - from initial recruitment through long-term development. Let's explore how to build and nurture a team that can turn your startup vision into reality.

Before diving into the specifics, let's visualize how the key elements of talent management work together in a scaling startup. These interconnected components form a continuous cycle of talent development and retention.

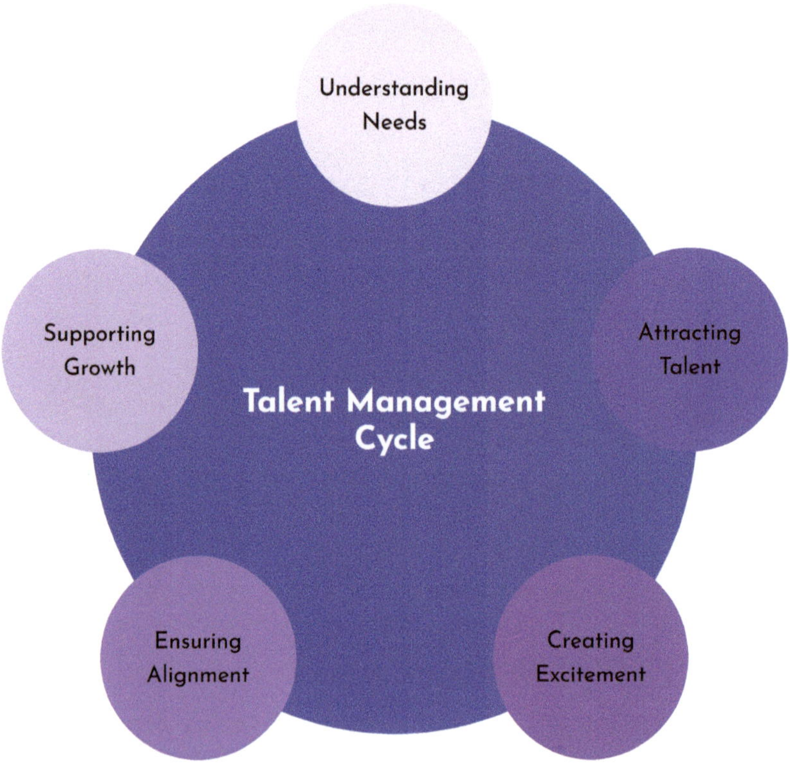

As illustrated in the diagram, talent management is a cyclical process where each element reinforces the others. Understanding needs (top) feeds directly into attracting talent (right), which leads to creating excitement (bottom right). This flows into ensuring alignment (bottom left) and ultimately supporting growth (left), which in turn helps us better understand our evolving needs. This continuous cycle ensures that your talent management strategy remains dynamic and responsive to your startup's changing requirements.

II. Building a Solid Foundation

The journey to building a stellar team begins long before writing your first job posting or reaching out to candidates. It starts with developing a deep understanding of your company's needs, culture, and vision. This foundational work is essential for making hiring decisions that will shape your startup's future.

Understanding your talent needs isn't just about listing required skills or experiences. It's about envisioning the future of your company and the people who will help you get there. As a founder, you must look beyond immediate vacancies and consider the long-term impact each new team member will have on your startup's culture and trajectory.

Here's how to approach this crucial foundation-building phase:

1. Define Your Company's Core Values and Culture Your company culture isn't just a set of perks or office norms – it's the underlying beliefs and behaviors that drive your organization. Before you can find people who will thrive in your environment, you need to clearly articulate what makes your culture unique.

2. Identify Key Roles and Competencies Once you've defined your culture, focus on identifying the key roles you need to fill and the competencies required for success in those roles.

3. Assess Your Current Team and Identify Gaps Before starting your hiring process, take stock of the talent you already have. This helps identify gaps and ensures you're building a well-rounded team.

4. Create Compelling Job Descriptions With a clear understanding of your culture, key roles, and current gaps, you can create job descriptions that will attract the right candidates.

   Tips for Effective Job Descriptions:

   - Start with an engaging company overview that highlights your mission and culture
   - Clearly outline responsibilities and expectations
   - List both required and preferred qualifications
   - Highlight growth opportunities and unique aspects of working at your startup
   - Use inclusive language to attract a diverse pool of candidates

5. Develop Your Employee Value Proposition (EVP) Your EVP is the unique set of benefits an employee receives in return for the skills, capabilities, and experience they bring to your company. A strong EVP can be a powerful tool in attracting top talent.

   Components of a Strong EVP:

   - Compelling mission and vision
   - Opportunities for growth and development
   - Competitive compensation and benefits
   - Positive work environment and culture

- Work-life balance
- Recognition and rewards

The Employee Value Proposition (EVP) can be visualized as a pyramid, with each layer building upon and supporting those above it. This hierarchical structure helps prioritize different aspects of your EVP while showing how they work together.

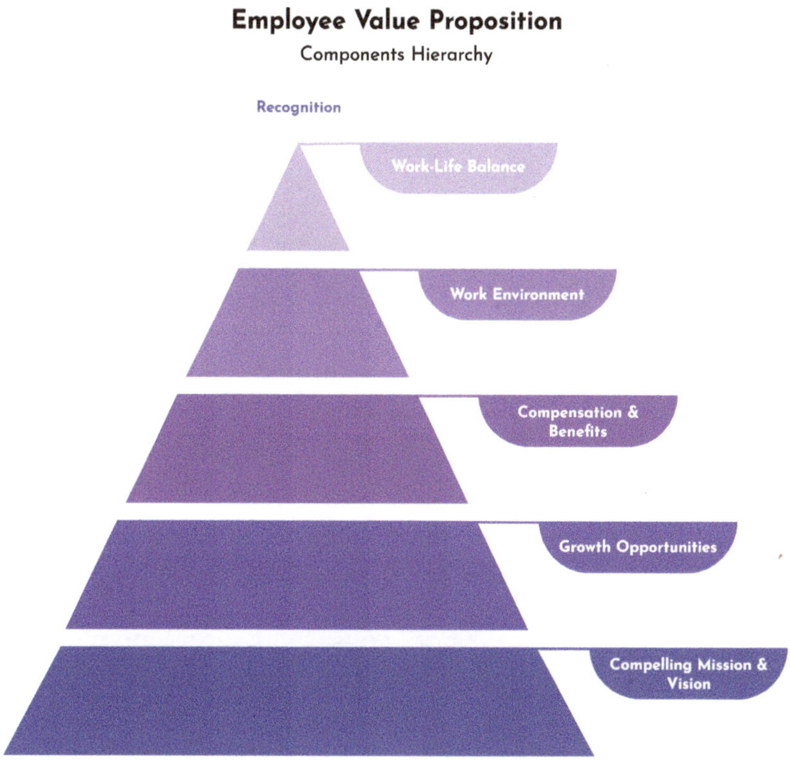

At the foundation of the pyramid lies your compelling mission and vision, providing the bedrock for everything else. This supports growth opportunities and competitive compensation, which together enable a positive work environment. Work-life balance builds upon this foundation, topped by recognition programs. Each layer depends on the strength of those below it - without a compelling mission, other benefits lose their impact. This structure helps explain why focusing solely on upper-level components (like recognition) without strong fundamentals often fails to attract and retain top talent.

Remember, as your startup scales, your needs will continually evolve. Make it a practice to regularly revisit and refine your understanding of your talent needs and culture. This ongoing process of self-reflection and definition will ensure that your team grows in a way that aligns with your vision and values.

III. Strategic Talent Acquisition

Once you've established a clear understanding of your talent needs and company culture, it's time to actively seek out the right candidates. In today's competitive startup landscape, passively waiting for talent to find you isn't an option. Success requires a proactive, creative, and strategic approach to finding the best people for your team.

Effective talent acquisition goes far beyond posting job listings and hoping for the best. It requires creating a comprehensive attraction strategy that positions your startup as an employer of choice.

To visualize how different sourcing channels work together, think of your talent acquisition strategy as a hub-and-spoke system, where various channels feed into a central coordination point.

In this model, the central hub represents your core talent acquisition function, coordinating efforts across all channels. Each spoke - job boards, employee referrals, social media, industry events, universities, and passive candidate outreach - serves a unique purpose. Notice how the channels are strategically positioned: complementary channels are placed near each other, and the size of each node reflects its typical impact on your talent pipeline. The connecting lines show how these channels must work in concert, often supporting each other in attracting the best candidates.

Here's how to approach this strategically:

1. Develop a Multi-Channel Sourcing Strategy Top talent can be found in many places, and you need to cast a wide net to find the right people. Consider these key channels:

   a) **Job Boards and Professional Networks**

   - Use both general (LinkedIn, Indeed) and industry-specific job boards
   - Leverage professional networks relevant to your industry

   b) **Employee Referrals**

   - Create an employee referral program with incentives for successful hires
   - Regularly remind employees about open positions and encourage referrals

   c) **Social Media**

   - Use your company's social media presence to showcase your culture and open positions
   - Encourage employees to share job openings on their personal networks

   d) **Industry Events and Meetups**

   - Attend or sponsor relevant industry events to meet potential candidates
   - Host your own meetups or workshops to attract talent

   e) **Universities and Bootcamps**

   - Build relationships with universities and coding bootcamps for entry-level talent

- Offer internships or apprenticeships as a pipeline for future full-time hires

f) **Passive Candidate Outreach**

- Use tools like LinkedIn Recruiter to identify and reach out to passive candidates who aren't actively job searching

2. Craft a Compelling Employer Brand Your reputation as an employer significantly impacts your ability to attract top talent. Building a strong employer brand is essential.

   Elements of a Strong Employer Brand:

   - Clear communication of your mission and values
   - Showcase of your unique culture and work environment
   - Highlighting of employee success stories and growth opportunities
   - Transparency about your company's challenges and how you're addressing them

   Exercise: Employer Brand Audit

   - Review your company's online presence (website, social media, review sites like Glassdoor)
   - Identify areas where you can better communicate your employer brand
   - Create a content calendar for sharing stories and insights that showcase your culture and opportunities

3. Leverage Content Marketing for Recruitment Content marketing can be a powerful tool for attracting talent, not just customers.

Ideas for Recruitment-Focused Content:

- Blog posts about your company culture and employee experiences
- Videos showcasing "a day in the life" at your startup
- Thought leadership articles demonstrating your company's expertise
- Behind-the-scenes looks at your product development process

4. Build a Talent Pipeline Don't wait for openings to start building relationships with potential candidates. A strong talent pipeline is invaluable.

Strategies for Building a Talent Pipeline:

- Create a database of interesting candidates you meet at events or through networking
- Stay in touch with promising candidates who weren't quite right for previous openings
- Engage with your wider network regularly to stay top-of-mind for potential referrals

5. Optimize Your Application Process After attracting potential candidates, ensure your application process doesn't create unnecessary barriers.

Tips for an Effective Application Process:

- Keep initial applications simple and quick to complete
- Ensure your careers page and application form are mobile-friendly
- Provide clear information about your hiring process and timeline

- Respond to all applications promptly, even if it's just an automated acknowledgment

Exercise: Application Process Audit Go through your own application process as if you were a candidate. Note any points of friction or confusion and work to streamline the process.

6. Engage in Proactive Outreach For key positions, take the initiative to reach out to potential candidates directly.

   Tips for Effective Outreach:

   - Personalize your messages based on the candidate's background and interests
   - Clearly articulate why you think they would be a good fit for your company
   - Provide specific information about the role and the impact they could have
   - Be prepared to "sell" your company and the opportunity

Success in talent acquisition requires being proactive and creative in your approach. In a competitive market, standing out is essential. By implementing a comprehensive sourcing strategy, building a strong employer brand, and engaging in proactive outreach, you can position your startup to attract exceptional talent that will drive your company's growth.

IV. Inspiring Candidates with Your Company's Vision and Opportunities

Once you've attracted potential candidates, the next crucial step in the UPGRADE Framework is to galvanize them – to inspire and excite them about the prospect of joining your startup. This stage is about more than just selling a job; it's about painting a vivid picture of the future you're building and the role they could play in shaping it.

The Galvanize stage is where your skills as a founder and visionary come to the forefront. Your ability to articulate your company's mission, convey its potential, and ignite passion in candidates can be the difference between hiring good employees and recruiting true believers who will go above and beyond to help your startup succeed.

A compelling company narrative follows a natural arc that takes candidates on a journey from understanding the problem you're solving to seeing themselves as part of your future impact.

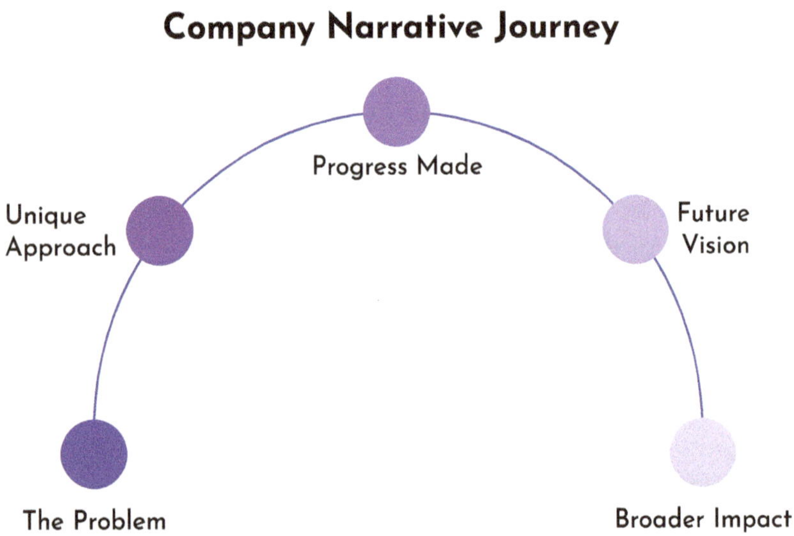

The arc diagram illustrates how your company's story flows from left to right, starting with the problem you're solving and building through your unique approach and current progress. Notice how the curve rises as the story develops, peaking at your vision for the future before connecting to the broader impact. This structure helps candidates see both the immediate opportunity and the longer-term potential of joining your team.

Here's how to approach the Galvanize stage effectively:

1. **Craft a Compelling Company Narrative**

   Your company's story is one of your most powerful tools for inspiring candidates. This narrative should go beyond what you do to why you do it and the impact you're striving to make.

   Elements of a Powerful Company Narrative:

   - The problem you're solving and why it matters
   - Your unique approach or solution
   - The progress you've made so far
   - Your vision for the future
   - The challenges you're facing and how you're addressing them

2. **Showcase Growth Opportunities**

   Top talent, especially in the startup world, is often motivated by the opportunity for rapid growth and development. Be clear about the growth opportunities your startup offers.

   Ways to Highlight Growth Opportunities:

   - Share stories of current employees who have grown with the company
   - Discuss your approach to professional development and learning
   - Explain how working at a startup provides unique

opportunities for wearing multiple hats and taking on significant responsibility

- If applicable, mention opportunities for equity or profit sharing as the company grows

3. **Provide a Window into Your Culture**

Culture can be a significant differentiator, especially for startups competing against larger, more established companies for talent. Give candidates a real sense of what it's like to work at your company.

Strategies for Showcasing Culture:

- Share stories that exemplify your company values in action
- If possible, give candidates a tour of your workspace
- Introduce candidates to team members in informal settings
- Be transparent about both the upsides and challenges of your culture

4. **Emphasize the Impact of the Role**

Help candidates understand the specific impact they could have by joining your team. This is especially important for startups, where individual contributions can have a significant effect on the company's success.

Ways to Highlight Role Impact:

- Clearly articulate how the role contributes to the company's overall mission
- Share specific projects or initiatives the person would be involved in

- Discuss how their work would affect customers or end-users
- If possible, provide metrics or goals that demonstrate the role's importance

5. **Address Candidate Concerns Proactively**

   Joining a startup often comes with certain risks or concerns for candidates. Address these proactively to build trust and demonstrate transparency.

   Common Concerns to Address:

   - Financial stability and funding status
   - Work-life balance expectations
   - Career progression in a flat organization
   - The company's plans for growth and potential exit strategies

6. **Leverage Your Network for Validation**

   Sometimes, hearing about your company from someone other than the founder or hiring manager can be powerful. If appropriate, connect candidates with other team members, advisors, or even customers who can speak to the value and potential of your startup.

   Ways to Use Your Network:

   - Arrange informal coffee chats between candidates and current employees
   - Share case studies or testimonials from satisfied customers
   - If you have notable advisors or investors, mention their involvement (with permission)

7. **Create an Immersive Interview Experience**

   Go beyond traditional question-and-answer interviews to give candidates a real taste of what working at your startup would be like.

   Ideas for Immersive Interviews:

   - Include a mini-project or problem-solving exercise relevant to the role
   - Invite candidates to attend a team meeting or brainstorming session
   - For technical roles, consider pair programming sessions
   - Offer a "day in the life" experience where candidates shadow team members

8. **Communicate Your Vision for the Future**

   As a founder, one of your most powerful tools for galvanizing candidates is your vision for the future. Share your big-picture plans and help candidates see how they could be part of something truly transformative.

   Elements to Include in Your Vision:

   - Long-term goals for the company
   - Potential new markets or products you plan to explore
   - How you see the company evolving as it scales
   - The broader impact you hope to have on your industry or society

Remember, the goal of the Galvanize stage is not just to fill a position, but to find people who will be truly excited and motivated to join your mission. By effectively communicating your company's story, opportunities, and vision, you can inspire candidates to see your startup not just as a potential employer, but as a vehicle for their own growth and impact.

V. Ensuring Mutual Fit

After generating initial excitement about your opportunity, it's crucial to ensure there's genuine mutual understanding and alignment between the candidate and your company. This validation process confirms there's a true fit – not just in skills and experience, but in values, expectations, and long-term goals.

The candidate validation process follows a systematic flow, with each step building upon the insights gained in previous stages. This ensures thorough evaluation while maintaining efficiency.

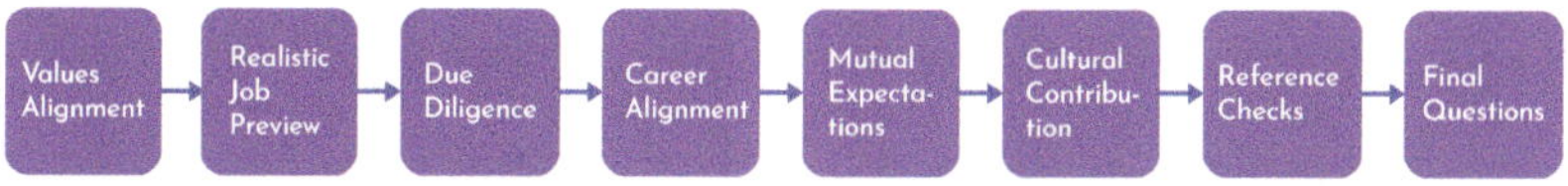

The flow diagram shows the eight critical steps in the validation process, from initial values alignment through to final questions. Notice how each step connects to the next, with clear progression and no shortcuts. The color coding indicates different aspects of validation - cultural (blue), technical (green), and organizational (orange) - ensuring comprehensive evaluation across all important dimensions.

Here's how to effectively validate candidate alignment:

1. Conduct In-Depth Values Alignment Interviews Beyond assessing skills and experience, dedicate time to exploring how well the candidate's values align with your company's culture.

Techniques for Values Alignment Interviews:

- Ask for specific examples of how the candidate has demonstrated values important to your company
- Present hypothetical scenarios that test cultural fit
- Discuss the candidate's ideal work environment and compare it to your culture
- Explore any potential conflicts between the candidate's values and your company's practices

2. Provide Realistic Job Previews While it's important to highlight exciting opportunities, it's equally important to give candidates a realistic preview of what the job entails, including its challenges.

   Elements of a Realistic Job Preview:

   - Typical day-to-day responsibilities
   - Common challenges or pain points in the role
   - Expectations for work hours and availability
   - The level of ambiguity or change they might experience
   - Any travel or location requirements

3. Encourage Candidate Due Diligence Empower candidates to do their own due diligence. This demonstrates transparency and helps them make informed decisions.

   Ways to Facilitate Candidate Due Diligence:

   - Provide access to company materials like annual reports or strategy documents

- Offer to connect candidates with current employees for candid conversations
- Be open to answering tough questions about your company's challenges or competitors
- If appropriate, share information about your company's financial health and funding status

4. Discuss Long-Term Career Alignment Ensure that the candidate's long-term career goals align with your startup's opportunities.

   Topics to Explore:

   - The candidate's career aspirations for the next 3-5 years
   - How the role and company could evolve as the startup grows
   - Potential career paths within the company
   - Opportunities for skill development and learning

5. Clarify Mutual Expectations Clear, mutual expectations are crucial for a successful long-term fit. Take time to explicitly discuss expectations on both sides.

   Areas to Cover:

   - Performance expectations and how they'll be measured
   - Communication styles and feedback processes
   - Decision-making processes and levels of autonomy
   - Work-life balance and flexibility
   - Compensation structure, including any equity components

6. Assess Cultural Contribution, Not Just Cultural Fit While cultural fit is important, also consider how a candidate might positively contribute to and enhance your culture.

   Questions to Consider:

   - What unique perspectives or experiences does the candidate bring?
   - How might they challenge your team to think differently?
   - What skills or knowledge could they share with the rest of the team?

7. Conduct Thorough Reference Checks Reference checks provide valuable third-party validation of a candidate's abilities and working style.

   Tips for Effective Reference Checks:

   - Go beyond the references provided by the candidate
   - Ask for specific examples of the candidate's performance and behavior
   - Inquire about areas where the candidate has room for growth
   - Validate key claims made during the interview process

8. Provide a Final Opportunity for Questions Before making an offer, give the candidate a final opportunity to ask questions or voice concerns.

This thorough validation process is crucial for preventing costly mis-hires. By deeply exploring alignment in values, expectations, and long-term goals, both your company and the candidate can make well-informed decisions about moving forward.

Remember, the goal isn't to only hire people who think exactly like you do. Diversity of thought and experience is valuable. The key is finding people who share your core values and vision while bringing fresh perspectives and ideas to the table.

VI. Nurturing Growth

Your responsibility to your team doesn't end when they accept a job offer - in fact, that's just the beginning. Building a successful startup requires creating an environment where your team can continuously grow, learn, and contribute at their highest level.

A successful onboarding program carefully sequences activities over the first 90 days, ensuring new hires build competence and confidence systematically.

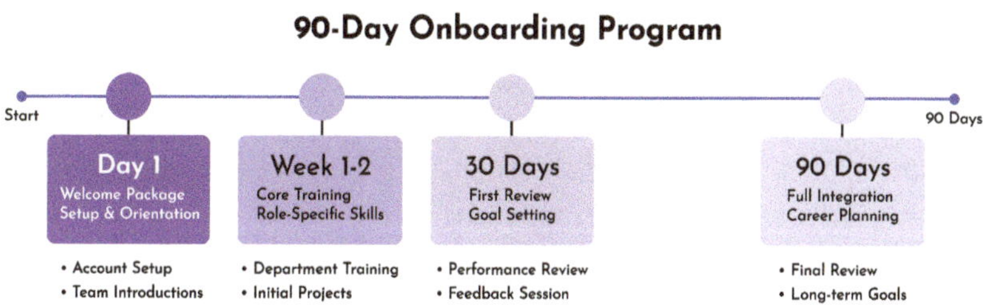

The timeline visualizes key milestones and activities across the 90-day journey. Notice how it progresses from immediate needs (Day 1 orientation) through role-specific training (Weeks 1-2) to broader integration (Month 1) and finally to full autonomy (Month 3). The color coding indicates the intensity of support needed at each stage, gradually decreasing as the employee becomes more independent.

Here's how to effectively nurture your team's development:

1. Create a Comprehensive Onboarding Program A strong

onboarding program significantly impacts an employee's long-term success and retention.

Key Elements of an Effective Onboarding Program:

- Pre-first day preparation (setting up accounts, preparing workspace, etc.)
- First day welcome and orientation
- Company history, mission, and values training
- Role-specific training and goal setting
- Introduction to key team members and stakeholders
- Regular check-ins during the first 30, 60, and 90 days

2. Implement Continuous Feedback Mechanisms Regular feedback is crucial for employee growth and alignment. Move beyond annual performance reviews to more frequent, informal feedback sessions.

   Continuous Feedback Strategies:

   - Weekly one-on-one meetings between employees and their managers
   - Monthly or quarterly performance check-ins
   - 360-degree feedback sessions
   - Real-time feedback tools or apps

3. Provide Opportunities for Learning and Development Investing in your employees' growth improves performance and increases engagement and retention.

   Learning and Development Ideas:

   - Allocate a personal learning budget for each employee

- Offer internal workshops or lunch-and-learn sessions
- Support attendance at relevant conferences and industry events
- Create a mentorship program
- Encourage cross-functional projects for skill development

4. Create Clear Career Progression Paths Even in a flat startup structure, employees should see opportunities for growth and advancement.

   Strategies for Career Progression:

   - Create clear job levels and criteria for advancement
   - Offer opportunities to lead projects or initiatives
   - Provide stretch assignments to develop new skills
   - Consider creating specialist or expert tracks for individual contributors

5. Foster a Culture of Innovation and Experimentation Encourage your team to innovate and take calculated risks. This drives company growth and provides valuable development opportunities.

   Ways to Foster Innovation:

   - Implement a "20% time" policy where employees can work on self-directed projects
   - Host regular hackathons or innovation challenges
   - Create a process for employees to pitch new ideas
   - Celebrate and learn from failures as well as successes

6. Prioritize Work-Life Balance and Well-being Burnout is a real risk in the high-pressure startup environment. Prioritizing employee well-being is crucial for long-term performance and retention.

   Well-being Initiatives:

   - Offer flexible working hours or remote work options
   - Provide mental health resources and support
   - Encourage regular breaks and vacation time
   - Implement wellness programs (e.g., gym memberships, meditation classes)

7. Regularly Reassess and Realign As your startup grows and evolves, so will your team's needs and role demands. Regular check-ins ensure ongoing alignment.

   Reassessment Strategies:

   - Conduct "stay interviews" to understand what keeps employees engaged
   - Regularly update job descriptions to reflect evolving responsibilities
   - Provide opportunities for employees to rotate roles or take on new challenges
   - Conduct annual skills gap analyses to identify development needs

Employee development is an ongoing process that requires consistent attention and investment. By creating an environment of continuous learning and growth, you not only improve the skills and capabilities of your team but also increase engagement, productivity, and retention.

Remember, in a startup, your team is your most valuable asset. The time and resources you invest in their development will pay dividends in innovation, productivity, and loyalty. By maintaining a strong focus on employee development and growth, you can build a world-class team capable of turning your startup vision into reality.

VII. Scaling Challenges

As your startup grows, you'll inevitably face several challenges in managing and developing your team.

As your startup scales, you'll encounter several common challenges in talent management. Understanding these challenges and their solutions helps you prepare proactively rather than react retroactively.

Scaling Challenges & Solutions

Challenge	Solution
Maintaining Culture Preserving startup culture during rapid growth	• Document and communicate values clearly • Make culture fit a key hiring criterion • Implement buddy system for new hires
Talent Competition Competing with larger companies for talent	• Emphasize unique startup benefits • Offer flexible work arrangements • Create compelling equity packages
Burnout Prevention Managing distributed teams effectively	• Invest in collaboration tools • Establish clear communication norms • Regular virtual team building
Remote Team Management Managing workload and stress levels	• Implement work-life balance policies • Provide mental health resources • Regular workload monitoring

The matrix pairs each major scaling challenge with specific, actionable solutions. Note how the solutions are practical and implementable, ranging from immediate actions (like documenting values) to longer-term strategies (like developing comprehensive training programs). The alternating colors help distinguish between different challenge categories while making the information easy to scan and reference.

Here are key challenges and practical strategies to address them:

1. Maintaining Culture as You Grow Challenge: During rapid growth phases, preserving your startup's original culture becomes increasingly difficult as new team members join.

   Solution:

   - Clearly document and communicate your company values
   - Make culture fit a key criterion in your hiring process
   - Implement a buddy system for new hires to help them acclimate to the culture
   - Regularly reinforce culture through team events, communications, and recognition programs

2. Balancing Immediate Needs vs. Long-term Potential Challenge: Urgent hiring needs can lead to prioritizing immediate skills over long-term potential.

   Solution:

   - Develop a strategic workforce plan that considers future needs

- Look for adaptable candidates with a growth mindset
- Implement a robust internal training program to develop needed skills
- Consider creating internship or apprenticeship programs to build a talent pipeline

3. Competing with Larger Companies for Talent Challenge: Startups often struggle to match the compensation packages offered by established companies.

   Solution:

   - Emphasize unique benefits of startup work (impact, growth opportunities, equity)
   - Offer flexible work arrangements or other non-monetary benefits
   - Develop a strong employer brand that showcases your company culture and mission
   - Consider creative compensation structures, like performance-based bonuses or equity

4. Managing Remote and Distributed Teams Challenge: Remoteworkbringsuniquechallengesincommunication, collaboration, and culture-building.

   Solution:

   - Invest in robust communication and collaboration tools
   - Establish clear communication norms and expectations

- Create opportunities for virtual social interaction and team building
- Consider occasional in-person meetups for distributed teams

5. Developing New Managers Challenge: First-time managers often struggle with their transition, particularly in fast-growing environments.

   Solution:

   - Provide management training and mentorship for new leaders
   - Clearly define expectations for managers in your organization
   - Offer ongoing support and resources for developing leadership skills
   - Consider hiring experienced managers to complement homegrown talent

6. Preventing Burnout Challenge: High-pressure startup environments can lead to burnout and turnover.

   Solution:

   - Promote a culture that values work-life balance
   - Provide mental health resources and support
   - Encourage time off and model good work-life balance from the top
   - Regularly check in with team members about their workload and stress levels

7. Addressing Underperformance Challenge: In small teams, underperformance has outsized impact but can be difficult to address, especially with early employees.

   Solution:

   - Set clear performance expectations from the start
   - Provide regular feedback and opportunities for improvement
   - Develop a structured performance improvement process
   - Be willing to make tough decisions if improvement doesn't occur

8. Retaining Top Performers Challenge: High-performing team members often become targets for recruiters as your startup gains visibility.

   Solution:

   - Regularly check in with top performers about their goals and satisfaction
   - Provide opportunities for growth and new challenges
   - Ensure compensation remains competitive
   - Recognize and reward exceptional performance

Remember that effectively managing talent requires constant attention and adaptation. By anticipating these common challenges and implementing proactive solutions, you can build and maintain a strong, engaged team that drives your startup's growth and success.

Blueprint Summary

Building a world-class team is fundamental to scaling success. The UPGRADE pillar focuses on creating systematic approaches to attracting, developing, and retaining exceptional talent. It's about building scalable processes that ensure your team grows in both size and capability while maintaining culture and performance.

Key Takeaways

1. **Talent Acquisition Strategy**
    - Develop diverse sourcing channels to find right talent
    - Design consistent and effective interview processes
    - Create objective candidate assessment frameworks
    - Build compelling employer brand narrative
    - Implement recruitment analytics for continuous improvement
2. **Onboarding Excellence**
    - Create structured 90-day integration plans
    - Develop clear role and responsibility definitions
    - Enable smooth culture integration for new hires
    - Build efficient knowledge transfer systems
    - Set clear performance expectations from start

3. **Performance Management**
    - Align individual goals with company objectives
    - Create regular feedback systems and dialogues
    - Implement structured evaluation processes
    - Design clear career development paths
    - Build recognition programs that reinforce success
4. **Learning & Development**
    - Conduct regular skill gap analysis
    - Provide structured training programs
    - Implement mentorship systems
    - Enable organization-wide knowledge sharing
    - Build strong leadership development pipeline
5. **Retention Strategy**
    - Measure and track employee engagement
    - Create meaningful growth opportunities
    - Maintain competitive compensation structures
    - Foster positive work environment
    - Ensure strong cultural alignment and connection

Conclusion

The ability to build and retain a high-performing team is perhaps the most critical factor in startup success. However, it's not enough to simply hire great people—you need systematic approaches to developing and retaining them. The most successful startups understand that talent management is not a series of one-off activities but a comprehensive system that needs to be carefully designed and continuously refined.

Your talent strategy must evolve as your company grows, starting with foundational elements like clear role definitions and basic onboarding processes, then growing into more sophisticated systems for development and retention. The key is to build scalable processes that can grow with your organization while maintaining the quality and culture that make your company special.

However, even the most talented team can only succeed with a clear product vision and effective product development processes. This brings us to Chapter 7: PRODUCT, where we'll explore how to channel your team's capabilities into building products that customers love. While having great talent is essential, the way you organize and direct that talent toward product development determines your ultimate success.

In the next chapter, we'll dive into creating product development processes that maximize your team's potential and ensure you're building the right things in the right way. We'll see how combining strong talent management with effective product development creates a powerful engine for innovation and growth. The synergy between great people and great product processes is what enables your startup to not just compete, but to dominate your market.

The transition from talent to product is natural—because ultimately, your ability to build great products depends on having great people working in effective ways. As we move from building the team to building the product, you'll learn how to create systems that enable your talented team to consistently deliver exceptional value to your customers.

Put These Ideas Into Action

Get your free unicorn Blueprint Field Guide with templates & worksheets

Scan the QR code or visit the URL below to access your resources
https://scaleupmethodology.com/the-unicorn-blueprint-fieldguide/

Chapter No. 7

PRODUCT: Craft Customer Obsessions

I. The Product Imperative in Scaling Startups

In the exhilarating journey of scaling a startup, it's easy to get caught up in the whirlwind of rapid growth, new hires, and expanding operations. However, amidst this chaos of scaling, one truth remains constant: your product is the heart of your business. It's what solves your customers' problems, what sets you apart from competitors, and ultimately, what will determine your long-term success.

As a founder, maintaining an unwavering focus on your product as you scale is both a challenge and a necessity. The challenge lies in balancing the myriad demands of a growing business with the need for continuous product innovation and improvement. The necessity stems from the simple fact that without a product that continues to delight customers and stay ahead of market needs, all other scaling efforts are futile.

Consider the cautionary tale of Jawbone, once a darling of the tech world valued at $3 billion. Despite raising nearly $1 billion in funding and scaling rapidly, Jawbone ultimately failed due to product issues. They lost focus on what customers truly wanted, released products with quality issues, and failed to innovate quickly enough in a competitive market. This story underscores a crucial lesson: scaling without a relentless focus on product excellence is a recipe for failure.

On the flip side, look at a company like Zoom. Their meteoric rise, especially during the COVID-19 pandemic, wasn't just about being in the right place at the right time. It was the result of years of focused product development, creating a video conferencing solution that was significantly easier to use than existing alternatives. Even as they scaled rapidly, Zoom maintained its focus on product quality and user experience, continually refining and improving their core offering.

The product imperative in scaling startups is clear: as you grow, your product must grow with you. It must evolve to meet the changing needs of your expanding customer base, adapt to new market conditions, and continue to outpace competitors. This requires not just maintaining your existing product, but continuously innovating, refining your approach to product development, and staying obsessively focused on delivering value to your customers.

In this chapter, we'll explore strategies for maintaining this crucial product focus as you scale. We'll dive deep into modern product development methodologies like dual-track agile, explore the critical role of ongoing product discovery, and discuss how to align your product roadmap with your overall company strategy. We'll look at how to leverage metrics for data-driven product decisions, how to maintain product-market fit in a changing landscape, and how to avoid common pitfalls that trip up many scaling startups.

Remember, as you scale, every other aspect of your business – your team, your operations, your culture – should ultimately serve one purpose: creating and delivering an exceptional product that solves real problems for your customers. Let's dive in and explore how to make this product obsession a reality in your scaling startup.

Before we dive deeper, let's visualize how product excellence integrates with and is supported by the other pillars of the Scaleup Methodology:

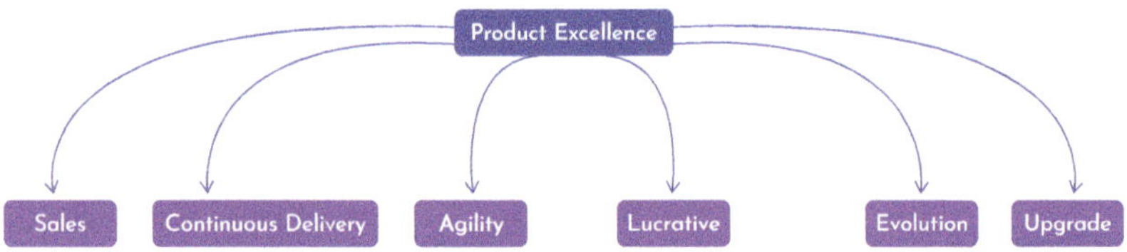

As shown in the diagram, Product Excellence sits at the center, supported by six critical pillars. The SALES pillar ensures your product reaches the right customers, while CONTINUOUS DELIVERY enables rapid and reliable product iterations. AGILITY allows you to adapt your product quickly to market needs, while the LUCRATIVE pillar ensures sustainable product economics.

The EVOLUTION pillar provides the organizational structure needed for product growth, and UPGRADE ensures you have the right talent to build exceptional products. Each pillar plays a vital role in product success, and their integration is key to scaling effectively.

II. The Evolution of Product Development in Scaling Startups

The journey from a fledgling startup with a Minimum Viable

Product (MVP) to a scaling company with a mature, feature-rich product is a transformative one. This evolution isn't just about adding more features or serving more customers – it's about fundamentally changing how you approach product development.

From MVP to Scalable Product

In the early days of a startup, the focus is on validating your core value proposition as quickly and cheaply as possible. This is the realm of the MVP – a product with just enough features to satisfy early customers and provide feedback for future development. The approach here is often scrappy and intuitive, driven by the founders' vision and direct interactions with early adopters.

I remember working with a fintech startup in their early days. Their MVP was a basic budgeting app with manual expense tracking. It wasn't pretty, and it lacked many features, but it was enough to validate that there was a real need for their solution. They built it in just two months and immediately got it into the hands of users.

As you start to scale, however, this approach no longer suffices. You need to move from a product that proves a concept to one that can support a growing user base, integrate with other systems, and evolve rapidly in response to market needs. This scalable product is more robust, more feature-rich, and designed with growth in mind.

For our fintech startup, this meant evolving their app to include automatic transaction importing from banks, advanced categorization algorithms, and data visualization tools. More importantly, they had to rebuild their backend to handle millions of users and transactions, implement robust security measures, and create APIs for future integrations.

The evolution from MVP to mature product follows a predictable pattern, though the specifics vary by company. Let's visualize this journey:

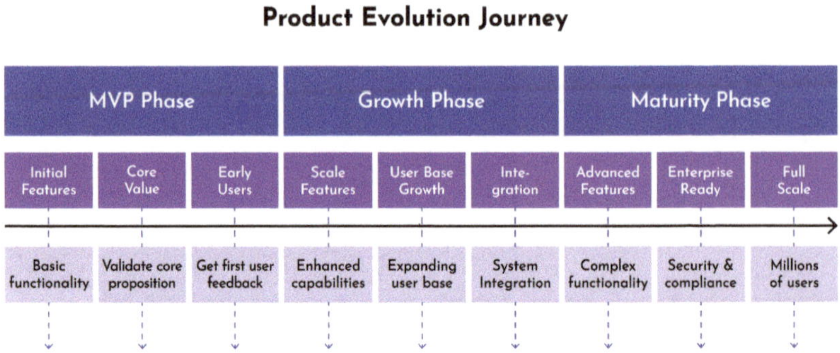

This timeline illustrates the three major phases of product evolution. Notice how each phase builds upon the previous one: the MVP phase focuses on core value and validation, the Growth phase emphasizes scaling and integration, and the Maturity phase introduces enterprise-grade features and capabilities. The increasing complexity at each stage reflects both the growing sophistication of your product and the expanding needs of your user base.

The Need for a More Structured Approach

As your product and team grow, the intuitive, founder-driven approach to product development becomes unsustainable. You need a more structured approach that can:

1. Accommodate input from a larger, more diverse set of stakeholders
2. Manage a more complex product with interdependent features
3. Balance new feature development with maintenance and technical debt

4. Ensure consistency and quality across a growing product surface area
5. Align product development with broader business strategies and goals

This is where more formal product development methodologies come into play. As we explored in detail in Chapter 3 (AGILITY), approaches like Agile, Scrum, and Kanban provide frameworks for managing the increasing complexity of product development in a scaling startup.

However, even these methodologies often fall short when it comes to balancing the need for continuous innovation with the demands of delivering a reliable, scalable product. This is where more advanced approaches, like dual-track agile, come into play.

Case Study: Spotify's Product Development Evolution

Spotify's evolution provides an excellent example of how product development changes as a startup scales. In their early days, Spotify focused on a simple, intuitive interface for streaming music. Their product development was primarily driven by the founding team's vision and direct user feedback.

As they scaled, they realized they needed a more structured approach that could accommodate their growing team and increasingly complex product. They developed their own agile framework, the "Spotify Model," which organizes teams into "squads," "tribes," "chapters," and "guilds." This model allowed them to maintain the agility of a startup while providing the structure needed for a large, complex organization.

Moreover, Spotify embraced a dual-track approach, with

dedicated teams for product discovery and delivery. This allowed them to continuously explore new features and improvements (like personalized playlists and podcast integration) while maintaining and scaling their core product.

The result? Spotify has been able to continuously innovate, regularly rolling out new features and improvements while scaling to serve over 350 million users globally. Their product development evolution has been a key factor in their growth from startup to industry leader.

As we move forward in this chapter, we'll explore in depth how you can evolve your product development approach to support your scaling startup, starting with the powerful framework of dual-track agile.

III. Dual-Track Agile

As startups scale, they often find themselves caught between two crucial imperatives: the need to continuously innovate and explore new ideas, and the demand to reliably deliver and improve their existing product. This is where dual-track agile comes in, providing a framework to balance these competing needs.

Understanding Dual-Track Agile

Dual-track agile is an approach to product development that separates work into two parallel tracks:

1. **The Discovery Track:** Focused on understanding user needs, exploring new ideas, and validating potential solutions.
2. **The Delivery Track:** Centered on building, testing, and shipping validated product increments.

While these tracks operate in parallel, they're deeply interconnected, with constant communication and feedback loops between them. This approach allows teams to maintain a steady pace of product delivery while simultaneously exploring new opportunities and innovations.

Let's visualize how the Discovery and Delivery tracks operate in parallel while maintaining crucial connections:

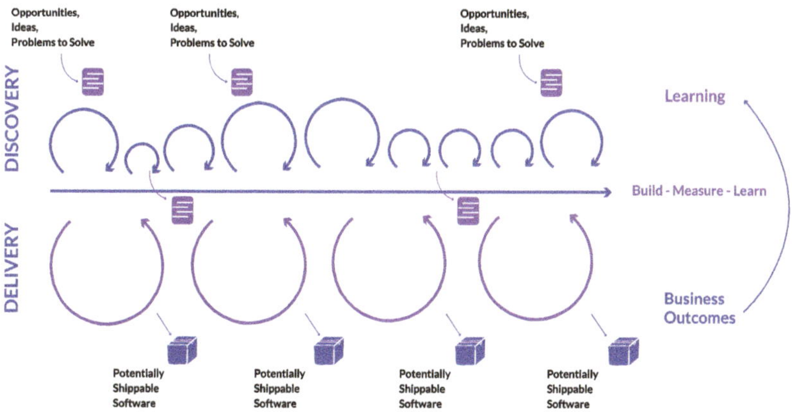

In this diagram, you can see how both tracks operate as continuous cycles. The Discovery track (in green) moves through Research, Ideation, Prototyping, and Validation, while the Delivery track (in blue) progresses through Planning, Building, Testing, and Deployment. The dotted line between Validation and Planning represents the crucial handoff point where validated ideas move into development. Notice how each track maintains its own rhythm while staying connected to the other.

The Discovery Track: Continuous Innovation and Validation

The discovery track is all about learning and risk reduction. It's where product managers, designers, and researchers work together to:

1. Understand user needs and pain points
2. Generate and explore new product ideas
3. Create and test prototypes
4. Validate assumptions about user behavior and preferences
5. De-risk potential solutions before committing to full development

The key to an effective discovery track is rapid learning cycles. Instead of lengthy research phases, teams work in short sprints (often 1-2 weeks) focused on validating specific hypotheses. This might involve activities like:

- User interviews and surveys
- Competitive analysis
- Paper prototyping
- A/B testing of design concepts
- Wizard of Oz testing for complex features

The goal is to quickly separate good ideas from bad ones, and to refine promising concepts until they're ready for development.

The Delivery Track: Efficient Execution and Scaling

The delivery track is where validated ideas are turned into reality. As we explore in depth in Chapter 2 (CONTINUOUS DELIVERY) and Chapter 3 (AGILITY), this track focuses on:

1. Building new features and products
2. Improving existing functionality

3. Ensuring product quality and reliability
4. Scaling the product to meet growing demand

The delivery track typically operates on a more structured cadence, leveraging the principles and practices detailed in our CONTINUOUS DELIVERY and AGILITY pillars.

Whether using methodologies like Scrum or Kanban, the key here is to maintain a steady, predictable pace of delivery while remaining flexible enough to incorporate new insights from the discovery track.

Implementing Dual-Track Agile in Your Startup

Implementing dual-track agile requires careful planning and a shift in mindset. Here are some steps to get started:

1. **Establish Dedicated Discovery Resources:** Allocate specific team members or even entire teams to focus on discovery work. This typically includes product managers, UX designers, and researchers.
2. **Create Clear Processes for Moving Ideas from Discovery to Delivery:** Develop a systematic approach for how ideas progress from initial concept through validation and into development. This might include stages like:
   - Idea generation
   - Initial validation
   - Prototyping and user testing
   - Business case development
   - Handoff to delivery teams
3. **Visualize Both Discovery and Delivery Work:** Use visual management tools like Kanban boards to track both discovery and delivery work. This provides transparency

and helps identify bottlenecks in the process.

4. **Balance Team Capacity Across Both Tracks:** Ensure that there's sufficient capacity in both discovery and delivery tracks. The ratio will depend on your specific needs, but a common starting point is allocating about 20-30% of capacity to discovery work.

5. **Foster Tight Collaboration Between Discovery and Delivery Teams:** While the work is separated into two tracks, the teams should not be siloed. Regular touchpoints between discovery and delivery teams ensure that insights are shared, technical feasibility is considered early, and the transition from discovery to delivery is smooth.

6. **Implement Rapid Learning Cycles:** In the discovery track, implement short learning cycles focused on validating specific hypotheses. This maintains momentum and ensures regular progress.

7. **Align Discovery Work with Strategic Goals:** Ensure that discovery efforts are guided by the startup's overall strategy and goals. This prevents the discovery track from becoming a disparate collection of ideas without clear business value.

Case Study: How We Implemented Dual-Track Agile at a Scaling Startup

I once worked with a B2B SaaS startup that was struggling to balance innovation with the demands of their growing customer base. They were caught in a cycle of reactively building features requested by their biggest clients, without a clear product vision or innovation pipeline.

We implemented dual-track agile, starting by forming a dedicated discovery team consisting of a product manager, a UX designer, and a user researcher. This team was tasked with looking beyond immediate customer requests to identify longer-term opportunities and pain points.

We set up a discovery kanban board with columns for "Ideas," "Researching," "Prototyping," "Validating," and "Ready for Development." The discovery team worked in one-week cycles, each focused on validating a specific hypothesis about user needs or potential solutions.

Meanwhile, the delivery team continued their two-week sprint cycles, but with a newly clarified backlog informed by the discovery team's findings. We established bi-weekly "bridge" meetings where the discovery and delivery teams would share insights and align on priorities.

The results were transformative. Within three months, the company had a clear product roadmap that balanced customer needs with innovative new features. They were able to launch two major new features that opened up new market segments, while still maintaining their existing product and keeping current customers happy.

More importantly, they had built a sustainable engine for continuous innovation and delivery. The discovery track ensured a steady stream of validated ideas, while the delivery track turned these ideas into reality at a predictable pace.

Implementing dual-track agile isn't without its challenges. It requires a shift in mindset, clear communication, and ongoing refinement. But for scaling startups looking to maintain their innovative edge while delivering a reliable product, it can be a game-changer.

In the next section, we'll take a deeper dive into the critical process of product discovery, exploring how to generate and validate product ideas that can fuel your startup's growth.

IV. Deep Dive In Product Discovery

Product discovery is the beating heart of innovation in scaling startups. It's the process of identifying and validating new product opportunities, ensuring that you're building the right things for your users and your business. As your startup scales, structured and continuous product discovery becomes increasingly crucial to maintain your competitive edge and continue delivering value to your growing user base.

The Importance of Ongoing Product Discovery

In the early days of a startup, product discovery often happens organically. Founders are close to their users, and the product evolves rapidly based on direct feedback and intuition. However, as you scale, several factors make ongoing, structured product discovery essential:

1. **Expanding User Base:** As you grow, you'll serve a more diverse set of users with varying needs. Continuous discovery helps you understand and address these evolving needs.

2. **Changing Market Conditions:** Markets change rapidly, especially in tech. Ongoing discovery helps you stay ahead of trends and adapt to new competitive landscapes.

3. **Avoiding Assumption Traps:** As your product matures, it's easy to fall into the trap of thinking you know what users want. Continuous discovery challenges these assumptions and keeps you connected to real user needs.

4. **Identifying New Opportunities:** Discovery isn't just about improving existing features; it's about finding entirely

new ways to deliver value to your users and expand your market.

5. **Reducing Risk:** By validating ideas before full development, you reduce the risk of investing resources in features that won't deliver value.

Key Components of Effective Product Discovery

Effective product discovery in a scaling startup typically involves the following components:

1. **User Research:** This includes both qualitative methods (like user interviews and usability testing) and quantitative methods (like surveys and usage data analysis).

2. **Market Analysis:** Understanding market trends, competitor movements, and emerging technologies that could impact your product.

3. **Idea Generation:** Structured processes for coming up with new product ideas and improvements, often involving cross-functional teams.

4. **Rapid Prototyping:** Creating quick, low-fidelity prototypes to test ideas before committing to full development.

5. **Experimentation:** Running controlled experiments to validate hypotheses about user behavior and preferences.

6. **Stakeholder Alignment:** Ensuring that discovery efforts are aligned with business goals and have buy-in from key stakeholders.

The following mind map illustrates how different elements of product discovery work together to create a comprehensive discovery process:

As visualized in the mind map, product discovery comprises five major areas: User Research, Market Analysis, Idea Generation, Validation, and Stakeholder Alignment. Each branch represents a crucial aspect of discovery, with specific activities and tools. Notice how User Research and Market Analysis inform Idea Generation, while Validation ensures ideas are viable before moving forward. Stakeholder Alignment runs parallel to all activities, ensuring business goals remain central to the discovery process.

Techniques for Generating and Validating Product Ideas

1. **Customer Journey Mapping:** Create detailed maps of your customers' experiences to identify pain points and opportunities for improvement.

2. **Jobs-to-be-Done Framework:** Focus on understanding the fundamental jobs your customers are trying to accomplish, rather than just their stated desires.

3. **Design Sprints:** Intensive, time-boxed sessions for rapidly designing, prototyping, and testing new ideas.

4. **Opportunity Solution Trees:** A visual tool for connecting high-level opportunities to concrete solutions and experiments.

5. **Lean Startup Experiments:** Apply the build-measure-learn cycle to quickly test hypotheses about your product and market.

6. **User Story Mapping:** A visual exercise used to build a shared understanding of how users interact with your product and where improvements can be made.

Case Study: Continuous Discovery at Spotify

Spotify's approach to product discovery offers valuable lessons for scaling startups. They use a combination of data analysis and qualitative research to continuously uncover user needs and preferences.

One of their key discovery techniques is the "Hack Week," where employees are encouraged to work on any project they believe could improve Spotify. Many features, like Spotify's popular Discover Weekly playlist, originated from these Hack Weeks.

Spotify also runs ongoing A/B tests on a massive scale, allowing them to validate new features and improvements with real users before full rollout. They combine this quantitative data with qualitative insights from user interviews and usability tests to build a comprehensive understanding of user needs and behaviors.

Connecting Product Discovery with Innovation Initiatives

Product discovery should not exist in isolation. To maximize its impact, it needs to be connected with broader innovation initiatives within your company. Here's how:

1. **Align Discovery with OKRs:** Ensure that your discovery efforts are guided by your company's Objectives and Key Results. This alignment ensures that innovation efforts contribute directly to your strategic goals.

2. **Feed Innovation Sprints:** Use insights from ongoing discovery to inform focused innovation sprints or hackathons. This allows you to dive deep into specific opportunity areas identified through discovery.

3. **Cross-Functional Collaboration:** Involve team members from different departments in discovery activities. This cross-pollination of ideas can lead to breakthrough innovations.

4. **Innovation Pipeline:** Create a clear process for moving ideas from initial discovery through validation and into your innovation pipeline for further development.

5. **Feedback Loops:** Establish mechanisms to feed learnings from innovation initiatives back into your ongoing discovery process. This creates a virtuous cycle of learning and innovation.

Product discovery is not a one-time activity, but an ongoing process that should be deeply embedded in your product development lifecycle. By implementing robust discovery practices, you ensure that your product continues to evolve in alignment with user needs and market opportunities, even as your startup scales rapidly.

In the next section, we'll explore how to translate these insights into a clear product roadmap that aligns with your company's strategic objectives.

V. Building a Product Roadmap Aligned with Strategy

A well-crafted product roadmap is the bridge between your company's high-level strategy and the day-to-day work of your product development teams. It provides direction and clarity, ensuring that everyone is aligned on what's being built, why it matters, and how it contributes to the company's goals. For scaling startups, where resources are precious and focus is crucial, an effective product roadmap becomes even more critical.

Translating OKRs into Product Initiatives

As we explored in Chapter 5 (EVOLUTION), translating strategy into action is a critical capability for scaling startups. One of the most effective ways to do this is by aligning your product roadmap with your company's Objectives and Key Results (OKRs). Here's how to make this translation:

1. **Start with Company OKRs:** Begin by thoroughly understanding your company's top-level OKRs. These should provide clear direction on what the company aims to achieve in the coming quarter or year.
2. **Derive Product OKRs:** Based on the company OKRs, create specific product OKRs. These should articulate how the product will contribute to achieving the company's objectives.
3. **Identify Product Initiatives:** For each product OKR, brainstorm potential initiatives that could help achieve that objective. These initiatives form the backbone of your product roadmap.
4. **Prioritize Initiatives:** Use a structured prioritization framework (like RICE - Reach, Impact, Confidence, Effort) to determine which initiatives should be pursued first.

5. **Map Initiatives to Timelines:** Based on your prioritization and resource constraints, map these initiatives onto a timeline. This forms the core of your product roadmap.

The following diagram illustrates the flow from high-level OKRs to actionable development tasks:

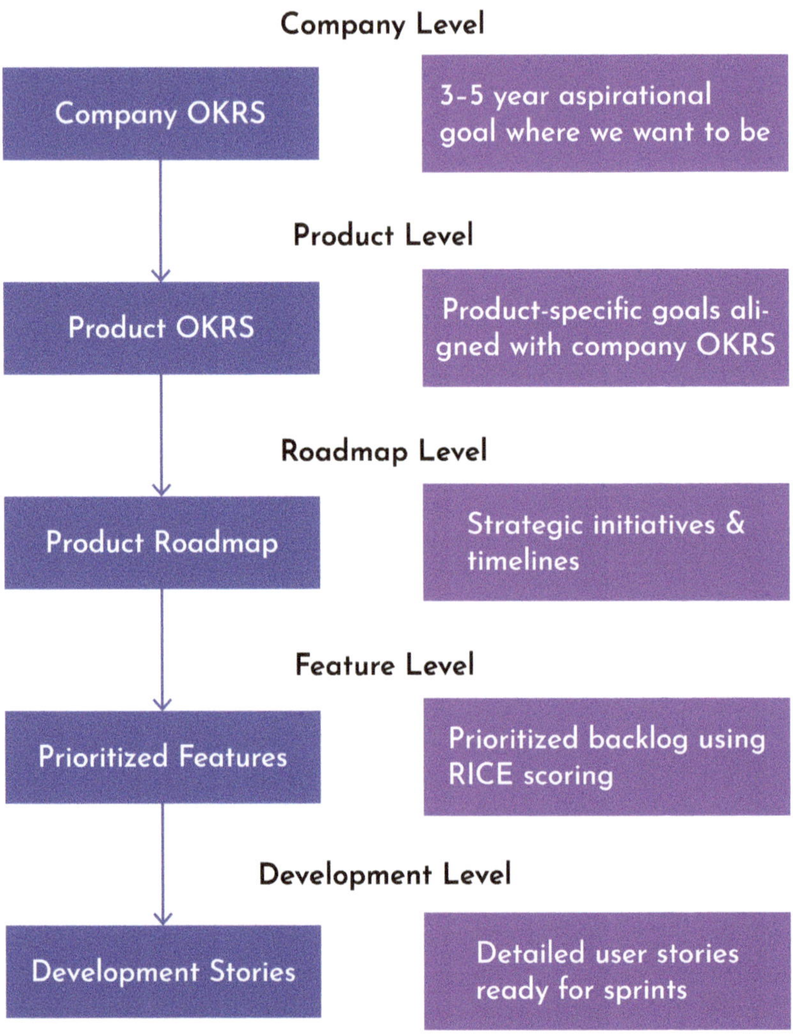

This hierarchy shows how we systematically translate strategic vision into actionable development work. At the top, Company OKRs set the strategic direction - for example, 'Increase market share in enterprise segment by 30%.' These cascade into Product OKRs that define how the product will contribute to these goals, such as 'Launch three enterprise-specific features with 80% adoption rate.'

The Product Roadmap then organizes these initiatives into a coherent timeline, mapping out when different capabilities will be delivered. This feeds into Prioritized Features - specific capabilities ranked by impact and effort - which are finally broken down into detailed Development Stories that development teams can execute in their sprints.

What makes this framework particularly powerful is its bidirectional nature. Not only does it help translate strategy into action, but it also allows teams to understand how their daily work connects back to larger company objectives. For instance, a developer working on a specific authentication feature can trace its lineage back to the company's strategic goal of enterprise market expansion.

Teams should regularly review their work against this hierarchy, asking questions like:

- Are our development stories clearly linked to prioritized features?
- Do our features align with roadmap initiatives?
- Are our roadmap initiatives directly supporting our Product OKRs?
- Are our Product OKRs meaningfully contributing to Company OKRs?

This consistent alignment checking helps ensure that effort at every level is contributing to strategic success.

Balancing Short-Term Wins with Long-Term Vision

One of the key challenges in product roadmapping for scaling startups is balancing the need for short-term wins with long-term strategic initiatives. Here are some strategies to achieve this balance:

1. **Use Time Horizons:** Structure your roadmap into different time horizons, such as:
    - **Now (next 3 months):** Highly specific, committed items
    - **Next (3-6 months):** Less specific, but high confidence
    - **Later (6+ months):** General direction, low specificity
2. **Allocate Resources Across Horizons:** Aim for a balance like 70% Now, 20% Next, 10% Later. This ensures you're making progress on long-term goals while delivering short-term value.
3. **Include Quick Wins:** Regularly include smaller, high-impact items that can be delivered quickly. These maintain momentum and provide visible progress.
4. **Revisit and Adjust Regularly:** Review and adjust your roadmap quarterly (or even monthly in fast-moving startups) to ensure it remains aligned with current priorities and market conditions.
5. **Communicate the Vision:** Always contextualize short-term initiatives within the broader product vision. This helps stakeholders understand how immediate work contributes to long-term goals.

Techniques for Prioritizing Product Features and Improvements

Effective prioritization is crucial for scaling startups, where resources are limited and making the right bets is critical. Here are some techniques to consider:

1. **RICE Scoring:** Prioritize based on Reach, Impact, Confidence, and Effort. This provides a quantitative way to compare different initiatives.

2. **Kano Model:** Categorize features as Must-haves, Performance, or Delighters. This helps ensure a balance between essential functionality and innovative features.

3. **Value vs. Complexity Quadrant:** Plot initiatives on a 2x2 matrix of value vs. complexity. Focus on high-value, low-complexity items first.

4. **Opportunity Scoring:** Based on the Jobs-to-Be-Done framework, this involves rating potential features based on their importance to users and current satisfaction levels.

5. **Buy-a-Feature:** A collaborative prioritization technique where stakeholders are given a limited budget to "buy" features. This surfaces what people value most.

6. **MoSCoW Method:** Categorize initiatives as Must-haves, Should-haves, Could-haves, and Won't-haves. This provides a clear hierarchy of importance.

Balancing Short-Term Wins with Long-Term Vision

One of the key challenges in product roadmapping for scaling startups is balancing the need for short-term wins with long-term strategic initiatives. Here are some strategies to achieve this balance:

1. **Use Time Horizons:** Structure your roadmap into different time horizons, such as:
    - **Now (next 3 months):** Highly specific, committed items
    - **Next (3-6 months):** Less specific, but high confidence
    - **Later (6+ months):** General direction, low specificity
2. **Allocate Resources Across Horizons:** Aim for a balance like 70% Now, 20% Next, 10% Later. This ensures you're making progress on long-term goals while delivering short-term value.
3. **Include Quick Wins:** Regularly include smaller, high-impact items that can be delivered quickly. These maintain momentum and provide visible progress.
4. **Revisit and Adjust Regularly:** Review and adjust your roadmap quarterly (or even monthly in fast-moving startups) to ensure it remains aligned with current priorities and market conditions.
5. **Communicate the Vision:** Always contextualize short-term initiatives within the broader product vision. This helps stakeholders understand how immediate work contributes to long-term goals.

Techniques for Prioritizing Product Features and Improvements

Effective prioritization is crucial for scaling startups, where resources are limited and making the right bets is critical. Here are some techniques to consider:

1. **RICE Scoring:** Prioritize based on Reach, Impact, Confidence, and Effort. This provides a quantitative way to compare different initiatives.

2. **Kano Model:** Categorize features as Must-haves, Performance, or Delighters. This helps ensure a balance between essential functionality and innovative features.

3. **Value vs. Complexity Quadrant:** Plot initiatives on a 2x2 matrix of value vs. complexity. Focus on high-value, low-complexity items first.

4. **Opportunity Scoring:** Based on the Jobs-to-Be-Done framework, this involves rating potential features based on their importance to users and current satisfaction levels.

5. **Buy-a-Feature:** A collaborative prioritization technique where stakeholders are given a limited budget to "buy" features. This surfaces what people value most.

6. **MoSCoW Method:** Categorize initiatives as Must-haves, Should-haves, Could-haves, and Won't-haves. This provides a clear hierarchy of importance.

A well-crafted, strategically aligned product roadmap is a powerful tool for scaling startups. It provides direction, aligns efforts across the organization, and ensures that your product development is directly contributing to your company's most important goals. By following these practices and regularly refining your approach, you can create a roadmap that not only guides your product's evolution but also drives your company's growth and success.

In the next section, we'll explore how to implement a metrics-driven approach to product development, ensuring that your product decisions are grounded in data and demonstrably driving your business forward.

VI. Metrics-Driven Product Development

In the fast-paced world of scaling startups, gut feelings and intuition are no longer enough to drive product decisions. As your company grows, it becomes crucial to implement a metrics-driven approach to product development. This ensures that your decisions are grounded in data, allowing you to measure the impact of your efforts and continuously improve your product.

Key Metrics for Product Success in Scaling Startups

The specific metrics you should track will depend on your product and business model, but here are some key categories and examples:

1. **User Acquisition Metrics**
    - Customer Acquisition Cost (CAC)
    - Time to First Value
    - Activation Rate
2. **User Engagement Metrics**
    - Daily/Monthly Active Users (DAU/MAU)
    - Session Length
    - Feature Adoption Rate
3. **User Retention Metrics**
    - Churn Rate
    - Customer Lifetime Value (CLV)
    - Net Promoter Score (NPS)

4. **Revenue Metrics**
    - Monthly Recurring Revenue (MRR)
    - Average Revenue Per User (ARPU)
    - Expansion Revenue
5. **Product Performance Metrics**
    - Load Time
    - Error Rate
    - Uptime

Let's visualize how different metrics categories contribute to overall product success and how quantitative and qualitative data work together:

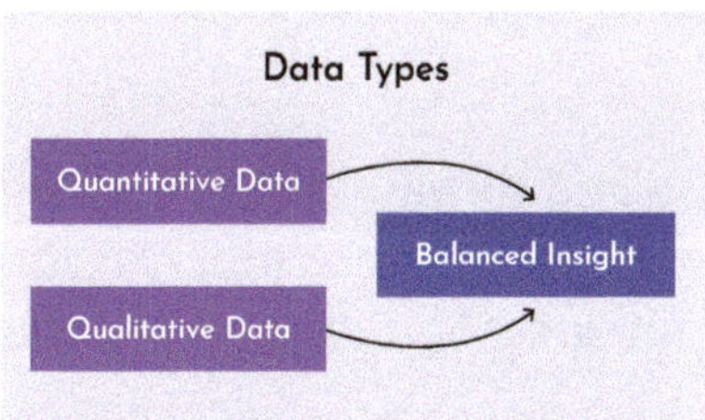

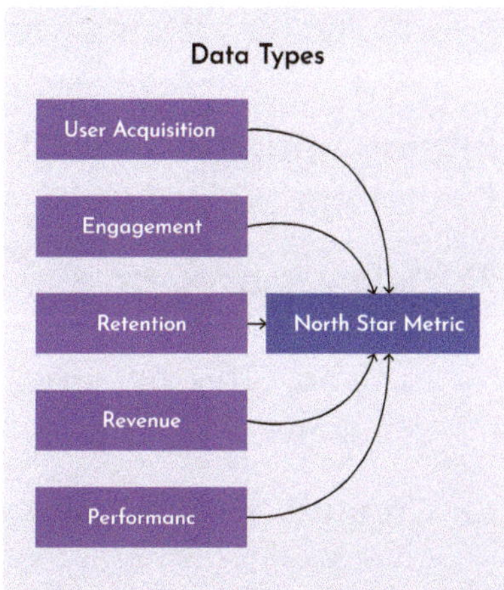

The diagram illustrates two key aspects of metrics-driven development. First, the top section shows how different metric categories (Acquisition, Engagement, Retention, Revenue, and Performance) feed into your North Star Metric. Below, we see how quantitative and qualitative data must be balanced to provide complete insight. Note how each metric category contributes unique information while working together to provide a comprehensive view of product performance.

Case Study: How Dropbox Uses Metrics to Drive Product Decisions

Dropbox, in its scaling phase, realized that user engagement was a key driver of their business success. They identified a metric they called "Magician's Moment" - the point at which a user has placed at least one file in their Dropbox folder on one device and viewed it on another device.

By focusing on this metric, Dropbox was able to optimize their onboarding process and product features to get users to this "aha moment" as quickly as possible. This metrics-driven approach contributed significantly to their rapid growth and high retention rates.

Implementing a Data-Driven Approach to Product Decisions

1. **Define Your North Star Metric:** Identify the one metric that best captures the core value your product delivers to users. This becomes your guiding light for product decisions.

2. **Create a Metrics Framework:** Develop a framework that links your North Star Metric to other supporting metrics. This helps you understand how different aspects of your product contribute to overall success.

3. **Set Up Analytics Infrastructure:** Implement robust analytics tools to collect and analyze user behavior data. Popular options include Google Analytics, Mixpanel, and Amplitude.

4. **Establish a Data Review Cadence:** Set up regular meetings (weekly or bi-weekly) to review key metrics and discuss their implications for product development.

5. **Use Data in Prioritization:** Incorporate metrics into your feature prioritization process. For example, you might prioritize features that are likely to have the biggest impact on your North Star Metric.

6. **Implement A/B Testing:** Use A/B testing to validate product changes before full rollout. This allows you to make data-driven decisions about new features or changes.

7. **Create Data Dashboards:** Develop easy-to-understand dashboards that make key metrics accessible to everyone in the organization.

Balancing Quantitative Data with Qualitative Insights

While quantitative metrics are crucial, they don't tell the whole story. It's important to balance these with qualitative insights:

1. **User Interviews:** Regularly conduct in-depth interviews with users to understand the "why" behind the numbers.

2. **Usability Testing:** Observe users interacting with your product to identify pain points and opportunities that might not be captured in the data.

3. **Customer Support Feedback:** Analyze support tickets and customer feedback for insights into user frustrations and desires.

4. **Survey Data:** Use surveys to collect structured qualitative feedback from a larger user base.

5. **User Session Recordings:** Tools like Hotjar allow you to watch recordings of user sessions, providing visual insights into how users interact with your product.

By implementing a metrics-driven approach to product development, scaling startups can make more informed decisions, allocate resources more effectively, and ultimately build products that better serve their users and drive business growth. Remember, the goal isn't to be driven solely by numbers, but to use data as a tool to inform and validate your product decisions.

In the next section, we'll explore how to maintain product-market fit as you scale - a crucial challenge for growing startups.

VII. Maintaining Product-Market Fit as You Scale

Achieving product-market fit is a significant milestone for any startup, but maintaining it as you scale is an ongoing challenge. As your user base grows and diversifies, as competitors enter the market, and as technology and user expectations evolve, what once was a perfect fit can begin to feel outdated or inadequate.

The Challenge of Evolving Product-Market Fit

Product-market fit isn't a static achievement; it's a dynamic state that requires continuous effort to maintain and evolve. Here are some of the challenges scaling startups face:

1. **Changing User Needs:** As you attract a broader user base, you'll encounter a wider range of needs and use cases.

2. **Market Evolution:** Markets can shift rapidly, especially in tech, changing what constitutes a good product-market fit.

3. **Competitive Pressure:** As you gain traction, competitors will emerge, potentially eroding your unique value proposition.

4. **Technical Debt:** As you've scaled quickly, you may have accumulated technical debt that limits your ability to adapt.

5. **Organizational Complexity:** As your team grows, it can become harder to stay connected to user needs and make rapid changes.

Strategies for Staying Connected to Customer Needs

1. **Regular User Research:** Implement a cadence of user interviews, surveys, and usability tests to stay in touch with evolving user needs.

2. **Customer Advisory Board:** Create a board of power users who can provide regular feedback on your product direction.

3. **Analytics Deep Dives:** Regularly analyze user behavior data to identify trends and changes in how your product is being used.

4. **Feedback Loops:** Implement multiple channels for gathering user feedback, from in-app feedback tools to social media monitoring.

5. **Employee Onboarding:** Have new employees go through the full user journey, providing fresh perspectives on the user experience.

6. **Executive User Interactions:** Ensure that executives and product leaders regularly interact directly with users.

Adapting Your Product to Serve New Market Segments

As you scale, you may find opportunities to expand into new market segments. Here's how to approach this expansion while maintaining your core product-market fit:

1. **Segment Analysis:** Conduct thorough research on the new segment to understand their specific needs and how they differ from your current users.
2. **MVP for New Segments:** Develop a Minimum Viable Product (MVP) tailored to the new segment, allowing you to test the market with minimal resource investment.
3. **Separate Teams:** Consider creating dedicated teams for new segments, allowing them to focus on segment-specific needs without disrupting your core product.
4. **Modular Architecture:** Design your product with a modular architecture that allows you to add or modify features for specific segments without affecting the core product.
5. **Tiered Offerings:** Consider creating tiered product offerings that cater to different segments while maintaining a consistent core experience.
6. **Continuous Validation:** Regularly validate that you're maintaining product-market fit across all segments you serve.

Maintaining product-market fit as you scale is a continuous process of listening, learning, and adapting. By staying closely connected to your users, analyzing market trends, and being willing to evolve your product, you can ensure that your solution remains relevant and valuable even as you grow to serve a larger, more diverse user base.

VIII. Continuous Business Model Refinement

As your product evolves and scales, it's crucial to continuously refine your business model to ensure it remains aligned with your product strategy and market realities. This ongoing refinement can be the difference between a startup that plateaus and one that achieves unicorn status.

The Interplay Between Product Development and Business Model

Your product and business model are intimately linked. Changes in one often necessitate changes in the other:

1. **Product Features Driving Business Model Innovation:** New product capabilities might open up new revenue streams or customer segments.
2. **Business Model Constraints Influencing Product Decisions:** Your pricing model or target customer might dictate certain product features or quality levels.
3. **Market Feedback Informing Both:** User behavior and market reception should inform both product development and business model refinement.
4. **Competitive Landscape Impacting Strategy:** Changes in the competitive environment might require adjustments to both your product and business model.

Case Study: How Slack Refined Its Business Model

Slack started with a straightforward per-user pricing model. However, as they grew and attracted larger enterprise customers, they realized this model wasn't optimal. They refined their business model in several ways:

1. **Introducing Enterprise Grid:** A new product tier for large organizations with different pricing and features.

2. **Implementing Fair Billing Policy:** Only charging for active users, which made Slack more attractive for large organizations with varying usage patterns.

3. **Creating an App Marketplace:** Opening a new revenue stream and enhancing the product's value proposition.

These refinements allowed Slack to better serve different customer segments and increase their revenue potential, all while staying true to their core product vision.

Techniques for Ongoing Business Model Innovation

1. **Business Model Canvas Reviews:** Regularly revisit your Business Model Canvas, questioning each component's relevance and exploring alternatives.

2. **Jobs-to-be-Done Analysis:** Continuously reassess the core jobs your customers are hiring your product to do. Are there new jobs emerging? Are you serving existing jobs optimally?

3. **Value Proposition Design:** Regularly review and refine your value proposition for different customer segments.

4. **Pricing Experiments:** Run controlled experiments with pricing changes to understand price sensitivity and optimize your pricing strategy.

5. **Customer Segment Expansion:** Continuously explore opportunities to expand into new customer segments, potentially with tailored offerings.

6. **Ecosystem Strategy:** Consider how you can create an ecosystem around your product (e.g., through APIs, partnerships, or marketplaces) to enhance value and create new revenue streams.

Aligning Product Strategy with Evolving Business Goals

As your business model evolves, it's crucial to ensure your product strategy remains aligned:

1. **Regular Strategy Sync Meetings:** Hold monthly meetings with product, sales, marketing, and finance leaders to ensure alignment between product direction and business goals.

2. **OKR Alignment:** Ensure product OKRs directly support the evolving business model and company-level OKRs.

3. **Product Roadmap Reviews:** Regularly review your product roadmap through the lens of your current business model and goals. Are you building the right things?

4. **Metrics Alignment:** Ensure your product metrics align with and support your key business metrics.

5. **Cross-Functional Product Teams:** Include team members from sales, marketing, and finance in product teams to ensure business perspective is always represented.

Continuous business model refinement is a critical practice for scaling startups. By regularly reassessing and innovating your business model, you ensure that your company remains adaptable, competitive, and aligned with evolving market needs. This ongoing refinement, coupled with strong product development practices, creates a powerful engine for sustainable growth and positions your startup for long-term success.

Blueprint Summary

Product excellence is the ultimate manifestation of all other pillars working in harmony. This chapter focuses on building systematic approaches to product discovery, development, and refinement that ensure you're creating solutions customers truly value. It's about establishing processes that consistently deliver exceptional products while maintaining the ability to innovate and adapt to changing market needs.

Key Takeaways

Product excellence represents the culmination of all other pillars working together effectively. The PRODUCT pillar focuses on creating systematic approaches to discovery, development, and refinement that ensure you're building solutions customers truly value. It's about establishing processes that consistently deliver exceptional products while maintaining the ability to innovate and adapt.

Key Takeaways

1. **Discovery Strategy**
    - Implement structured user research and feedback loops
    - Create systematic validation processes for new ideas
    - Establish clear criteria for moving ideas to development
    - Maintain continuous market and competitor analysis
2. **Development Process**
    - Implement dual-track agile for balanced innovation and delivery

- Create clear handoff processes between discovery and delivery
- Establish quality standards and testing protocols
- Maintain technical excellence through scalable architecture

3. **Product Strategy**

- Align product roadmap with company OKRs
- Implement data-driven prioritization frameworks
- Create clear success metrics for product initiatives
- Balance short-term wins with long-term vision

4. **Metrics Framework**

- Define and track key product performance indicators
- Implement comprehensive analytics infrastructure
- Create regular review cycles for product metrics
- Establish clear feedback loops for continuous improvement

5. **Market Fit Evolution**

- Monitor and maintain product-market fit as you scale
- Create systems for continuous customer feedback
- Adapt product strategy based on market changes
- Build scalable solutions for new market segments

These five elements create a comprehensive system for product development and innovation. Each component supports the others, creating an environment where great products can be consistently developed and improved. Success requires attention to all these elements while maintaining flexibility to adapt to changing market needs. This systematic approach enables organizations to build products that customers love while maintaining the ability to innovate and scale effectively.

Conclusion

Product excellence represents the culmination of all the previous pillars working together effectively. It's where your digital sales engine, continuous delivery capabilities, agile practices, financial acumen, organizational structure, and talented team come together to create real value for customers. The most successful startups understand that product development is not just about building features—it's about creating a systematic approach to understanding and solving customer problems.

Your product strategy must be both visionary and practical, combining long-term thinking with immediate execution. Start with fundamental elements like clear product vision and basic discovery processes, then build toward more sophisticated systems for innovation and scale. The key is to create repeatable processes that consistently deliver value while maintaining the ability to innovate and adapt.

This chapter concludes our exploration of the seven pillars of the Scaleup Methodology, but it represents just the beginning of your scaling journey. Each pillar we've covered—SALES, CONTINUOUS DELIVERY, AGILITY, LUCRATIVE, EVOLUTION, UPGRADE, and PRODUCT—provides essential capabilities that your startup needs to scale successfully. Together, they form a comprehensive framework for building a company that can achieve and sustain rapid growth.

The path forward involves implementing these pillars in your own context, adapting them to your specific challenges and opportunities. Success requires not just understanding these concepts but actively applying them, measuring their impact, and continuously refining your approach. Remember that scaling is not a destination but a journey of continuous improvement and adaptation.

As you move forward with implementation, keep in mind that these pillars are interdependent—strength in one area reinforces the others, while weakness in one area can undermine the whole. Focus on building foundational capabilities across all pillars while maintaining balance and alignment. Your goal is not perfection but progressive improvement that enables sustainable growth.

The journey to unicorn status is challenging but achievable with the right framework and mindset. By systematically implementing these seven pillars, you're building not just a successful startup, but a company capable of transforming its industry and creating lasting value for customers, employees, and stakeholders alike.

Put These Ideas Into Action

Get your free unicorn Blueprint Field Guide with templates & worksheets

Scan the QR code or visit the URL below to access your resources
https://scaleupmethodology.com/the-unicorn-blueprint-fieldguide/

Conclusion:

Building Unicorns, Changing the World

Imagine standing at the edge of a new frontier, where the next decade of innovation and entrepreneurship stretches out before us like an unexplored landscape full of possibility. Every successful startup that scales isn't just building a business – it's lighting a beacon of hope that illuminates the path for countless others to follow. Each unicorn we build becomes a constellation in an ever-expanding universe of human achievement, showing others what's possible when vision meets systematic execution.

Think of the entrepreneurs throughout history who transformed their industries and changed how we live – from Thomas Edison illuminating our world to Steve Jobs putting computers in our pockets. They didn't just build companies; they created ripples of innovation that continue to shape our future. Today, you stand at a similar threshold of possibility. But unlike those pioneers who had to find their way through trial and error, you hold in your hands a methodology forged from the successes and failures of thousands of startups, tested and refined in the crucible of real-world scaling. This isn't just about building another successful company – it's about being part of a movement that's redefining what's possible in the startup world.

The Seven Pillars: A Framework for Success

As we've explored throughout this book, the Scaleup Methodology rests on seven fundamental pillars, each critical to building a world-class organization:

1. **SALES**: Conquering the digital frontier with data-driven strategies
    - Building robust digital sales funnels
    - Creating content that drives engagement
    - Implementing metrics-driven optimization
2. **CONTINUOUS DELIVERY**: Unleashing engineering excellence
    - Automating deployment processes
    - Implementing robust testing strategies
    - Creating scalable architecture
3. **AGILITY**: Flexing, adapting, and dominating your market
    - Embracing rapid iteration
    - Building responsive teams
    - Fostering a culture of continuous improvement
4. **LUCRATIVE**: Unlocking financial mastery for sustainable growth
    - Implementing robust financial controls
    - Optimizing unit economics
    - Creating sustainable revenue models

5. **EVOLUTION**: Architecting your startup empire
    - Designing scalable organizational structures
    - Building effective communication channels
    - Creating systems for continuous learning
6. **UPGRADE**: Attracting and retaining superstar talent
    - Developing compelling employer brands
    - Creating growth opportunities
    - Building high-performance cultures
7. **PRODUCT**: Crafting customer obsessions that drive loyalty
    - Understanding user needs deeply
    - Iterating based on feedback
    - Building features that matter

Your Role in the Startup Revolution

The power of the Scaleup Methodology lies in its ability to serve different stakeholders in the startup ecosystem. Let's explore how each group can leverage these insights to drive meaningful change:

For Founders

You are the primary architects of innovation. Your next steps:

1. **Immediate Actions**
    - Take the Scaleup Assessment to benchmark your current state
    - Identify your three most critical gaps across the seven pillars
    - Create a 90-day action plan focusing on these gaps

2. **Short-term Implementation (3-6 months)**
    - Build your digital sales engine using the frameworks from Chapter 1
    - Implement the continuous delivery practices from Chapter 2
    - Begin organizational restructuring based on Chapter 5's guidance
3. **Long-term Strategy (6-12 months)**
    - Develop your talent attraction and retention strategy
    - Create your product evolution roadmap
    - Build your financial scaling model

For Accelerators and Incubators

You are the catalysts of startup success. Your opportunity:

1. **Program Enhancement**
    - Integrate the Scaleup Methodology into your curriculum
    - Develop metrics to track portfolio companies across all seven pillars
    - Create specialized workshops for each pillar
2. **Portfolio Support**
    - Implement regular scaling readiness assessments
    - Provide targeted mentorship aligned with the methodology
    - Create peer learning groups focused on specific pillars

3. **Ecosystem Building**
    - Partner with other accelerators to share best practices
    - Build relationships with investors who understand the methodology
    - Create regional communities of practice

For Investors

You are the fuel for startup growth. Your action items:

1. **Due Diligence Enhancement**
    - Use the seven pillars as an evaluation framework
    - Look for evidence of systematic scaling approaches
    - Assess leadership team's understanding of scaling principles
2. **Portfolio Support**
    - Help portfolio companies implement the methodology
    - Connect companies with relevant experts for each pillar
    - Create value-add programs aligned with the methodology
3. **Investment Strategy**
    - Develop thesis around systematic scaling
    - Build networks of co-investors who share this approach
    - Create funding structures that support methodical scaling

For Mentors and Consultants

You are the guides and enablers. Your pathway:

1. **Skill Development**
    - Deep dive into each pillar's frameworks and tools
    - Develop expertise in specific pillars that match your background
    - Build real-world case studies of methodology implementation
2. **Client Engagement**
    - Use the Scaleup Assessment as an engagement tool
    - Create pillar-specific consulting offerings
    - Develop implementation playbooks for different company stages
3. **Knowledge Sharing**
    - Contribute to the methodology's evolution
    - Share implementation stories and lessons learned
    - Build communities of practice around specific pillars

The Power of Integration

What makes the Scaleup Methodology particularly powerful is how these pillars work together. A strong sales strategy needs robust product delivery to succeed. Financial mastery requires the right talent to execute. Agility depends on proper organizational structure. When implemented thoughtfully and systematically, these pillars form an integrated system capable of turning promising ventures into world-changing unicorns.

Your Journey Continues

Your journey doesn't have to end with the last page of this book. The Unicorn Blueprint is more than just a methodology—it's an ecosystem designed to support your growth at every stage:

1. **Assess Your Starting Point**: Take the Scaleup Assessment to discover where your startup stands on each of the seven pillars and get personalized recommendations for improvement. Visit scaleup-scorecard.com to get started.

2. **Deepen Your Understanding**: Download The Unicorn Blueprint Field Guide - your practical workbook filled with templates, exercises, and implementation tools to put the Scaleup Methodology into action in your startup. Visit https://scaleupmethodology.com/the-unicorn-blueprint-fieldguide/ to get access.

3. **Join the Community**: Tune into "Scaleup Methodology Podcast" for in-depth discussions, expert interviews, and real-world case studies that bring the methodology to life. Visit scaleupmethodology.com/podcast to get started.

4. **Accelerate Your Growth**: Ready to turn these insights into action? Join us for the intensive Scaleup Bootcamp, where you'll work directly with scaling experts to create a customized roadmap for your startup's growth. As part of our commitment to community,, this transformative experience is offered free of charge to selected companies. Visit scaleupmethodology.com/bootcamp/ to learn more and apply.

A Vision of Revolutionary Change

The potential impact of improving startup success rates cannot be overstated. Imagine a world where instead of 9 out of 10 startups failing, we could flip that statistic on its head. The innovation, job creation, and economic growth that would result would be nothing short of revolutionary. By providing a clear, actionable framework for scaling, the Scaleup Methodology aims to make this vision a reality.

The Time for Action is Now

The future belongs to those who can not only envision it but build it. With the Scaleup Methodology as your guide, you have the tools to turn your startup dreams into unicorn realities. The question is no longer "Can we build a unicorn?" but "How quickly can we get there?"

Your role in this transformation is crucial. Whether you're leading a startup, working in one, or investing in the next generation of unicorns, you have the power to contribute to this transformation. Every successful implementation of these principles brings us closer to a world where startup success is the norm, not the exception.

So, are you ready to rewrite the rules of startup success? Are you prepared to join the ranks of founders who are not just building companies, but reshaping industries and changing the world?

Your unicorn journey starts now. Let's build something extraordinary together.

Acknowledgements

Every transformative journey begins with a vision, but it's the people who believe in that vision who help turn it into reality. This book, "The Unicorn Blueprint," represents not just years of experience and learning, but the collective wisdom and support of an extraordinary global community of innovators, entrepreneurs, and dreamers.

The vibrant startup ecosystems of Lisbon and Riyadh have been both laboratories and launch pads for the Scaleup Methodology. The energy, ambition, and innovative spirit I've encountered in these two dynamic cities have fundamentally shaped my understanding of what's possible in the modern startup landscape. The blend of European innovation and Middle Eastern transformation has provided an extraordinary perspective on scaling success.

I am particularly indebted to my mentors who have profoundly influenced my journey, Raphael B. and Ezequiel Vasconcellos, your wisdom, guidance, and unwavering support have been instrumental in shaping not just this methodology, but my entire approach to startup transformation. Your ability to challenge conventional thinking while maintaining practical focus has been invaluable.

To the countless startup founders who have trusted me with their dreams, allowed me to test and refine these concepts, and provided the real-world validation that has made this methodology robust and practical - your successes and even your setbacks have been invaluable teachers. Your courage to dream big and persevere through challenges continues to inspire me every day.

I'm profoundly grateful to the global network of mentors, clients, and friends who have contributed to this journey. From Lisbon's historic streets to Riyadh's modern boulevards, your diverse perspectives and experiences have helped create a truly universal framework for startup success. The conversations, challenges, and insights you've shared have been instrumental in shaping this methodology.

To the teams and organizations in both cities who have embraced and helped refine these concepts - your willingness to experiment, adapt, and share your learnings has been crucial in making this methodology practical and effective across different contexts and cultures.

To my family, who have supported this global journey with unwavering patience and understanding - your love and support have made this possible. And to my team at Evolution4all, whose dedication to helping startups succeed has been nothing short of remarkable - your commitment to excellence continues to inspire me.

Finally, to every entrepreneur who picks up this book with the dream of building something extraordinary - this is for you. May this blueprint help you turn your startup vision into a unicorn reality, creating value and changing lives across the globe.

The journey to reimagine startup success has just begun. Together, we can create a world where entrepreneurial success becomes the rule rather than the exception. Let's build something extraordinary together.

With gratitude and optimism for the future we'll build together, Luis Gonçalves

The Author

Luis Gonçalves is an experienced Digital Product Development specialist. Creator of the Scaleup Methodology and ADAPT Methodology®, he has helped numerous companies in building great digital products and becoming references in their industry. A bestselling author of "ADAPT", "Organisational Mastery" and "Product First," Through his work as a consultant, author, and speaker, he has influenced several companies worldwide in their journeys.

https://luis-goncalves.com

www.facebook.com/lmsgoncalves

www.linkedin.com/in/luismsg

www.twitter.com/lgoncalve1979

@luisgoncalves.e4all

Glossary

A

Agile: A methodology emphasizing iterative development, team collaboration, and adaptability to change. One of the seven pillars of the Scaleup Methodology focused on creating flexible, responsive organizations.

Annual Recurring Revenue (ARR): The yearly value of subscription-based revenue, calculated by multiplying Monthly Recurring Revenue (MRR) by 12.

B

Burn Rate: The rate at which a startup spends its cash reserves, typically measured monthly.

Business Model Canvas: A strategic planning tool that helps visualize, design, and update business models.

C

Canary Release: A technique for reducing the risk of introducing a new software version in production by slowly rolling out the change to a small subset of users before making it available to everyone.

Communities of Practice (CoPs): Groups within an organization that share expertise and passion for specific domains, fostering learning and innovation through regular interaction.

Continuous Delivery: One of the seven pillars of the Scaleup Methodology focused on reliably delivering software through automated testing and deployment processes.

Customer Acquisition Cost (CAC): The total cost of acquiring a new customer, including marketing and sales expenses.

Customer Lifetime Value (CLV/LTV): The total revenue a business can expect from a single customer account over the business relationship duration.

D

Design Sprint: A time-constrained, five-phase process for answering critical business questions through design, prototyping, and testing with customers.

Dual-Track Agile: A product development approach that separates work into two parallel tracks: discovery (understanding what to build) and delivery (building it).

E

Employee Value Proposition (EVP): The unique set of benefits employees receive in return for their skills, capabilities, and experience they bring to a company.

Evolution: One of the seven pillars of the Scaleup Methodology focused on creating scalable organizational structures and processes.

F

Feature Flag: A technique that allows teams to modify system behavior without changing code, enabling controlled rollout of features.

I

Impediment Board: A visual management tool used to track and resolve organizational obstacles and challenges.

J

Jobs-to-be-Done Framework: A methodology for understanding customer needs by focusing on the fundamental jobs customers are trying to accomplish.

L

Lean Budgeting: A funding approach that replaces annual departmental budgets with more flexible, value-stream-based funding models.

Lucrative: One of the seven pillars of the Scaleup Methodology focused on financial management and sustainability.

M

Minimum Viable Product (MVP): The version of a product with just enough features to test core assumptions with early customers.

Monthly Recurring Revenue (MRR): The predictable revenue a company expects to earn each month from subscription customers.

N

Net Promoter Score (NPS): A metric for measuring customer satisfaction and loyalty based on likelihood to recommend.

North Star Metric: The single metric that best captures the core value a product delivers to customers.

O

OKRs (Objectives and Key Results): A goal-setting framework that helps organizations define and track objectives and their outcomes.

P

Product Discovery: The process of validating product ideas and determining what to build through research, experimentation, and user feedback.

Product-Market Fit: The degree to which a product satisfies strong market demand and meets user needs effectively.

R

RICE Framework: A prioritization method considering Reach, Impact, Confidence, and Effort to evaluate product initiatives.

Runway: The amount of time until a company runs out of cash, assuming current income and expense levels stay constant.

S

Sales: One of the seven pillars of the Scaleup Methodology focused on building effective digital sales engines and customer acquisition processes.

Scaleup Methodology: A comprehensive framework for scaling startups comprising seven pillars: Sales, Continuous Delivery, Agility, Lucrative, Evolution, Upgrade, and Product.

U

Unicorn: A privately held startup company valued at over $1 billion.

Upgrade: One of the seven pillars of the Scaleup Methodology focused on talent acquisition and development.

V

Value Stream: The end-to-end series of activities that deliver value to customers, from initial concept through delivery and support.

Value Stream Funding: A financial approach that allocates resources based on value streams rather than traditional departments.

Also By This Author

www.ingramcontent.com/pod-product-compliance
Ingram Content Group UK Ltd.
Pitfield, Milton Keynes, MK11 3LW, UK
UKHW050710100225
4517UKWH00008B/47

9 783982 702322